Call to Mission

Call

to

Mission

by

STEPHEN NEILL

FORTRESS PRESS

PHILADELPHIA

Library of Congress Catalog Card Number 77–116460

COPYRIGHT © 1970 BY FORTRESS PRESS

2680B70   Printed in U.S.A.   1–217

BV
2061
N413
1970

Contents

1

Why Missions?

The missionary work of the Christian Church is a fact of the modern world. We may like the fact or we may dislike it. That makes no difference; whether we will or no, it is just there. Not only so; it is a large and ever expanding fact. A hundred years ago there were perhaps four thousand Protestant missionaries, including the wives of missionaries, in all the world and a rather larger number of Roman Catholics. The latest figures suggest that today we must reckon with at least forty thousand Protestant missionaries and about an equal number of Roman Catholics; this means that the missionary enterprise has multiplied itself tenfold in a hundred years. This is a reality which it is impossible for Americans in particular to disregard. More than half the Protestant missionaries in the world are citizens of the United States—about twenty-two thousand as against eighteen thousand from all the rest of the world put together. Until comparatively recently the Roman Catholic Church regarded the United States as a mission field—not as a country which could itself send out missionaries, but as one to which missionaries needed to be sent. Now all that is changed. The one particularly American Order of the Maryknoll Fathers, with its corresponding Order of Sisters, is now sending out missionaries to many parts of the world.

Then, too, for every missionary overseas there are at least five colleagues indigenous to the country in which he works—from bishops and church presidents through nurses and hospital attendants down to the ill-trained and under-paid village catechist on whom so much of the work of the church depends. So here is an army of devoted people, at it day and night in every corner of the world, concerned about one thing only—the message of Jesus Christ and getting it across to all kinds of people speaking a multitude of languages and living on every possible level of culture and civilization. In consequence you cannot travel far to-day, even in the heart of Africa, without coming across some traces of missionary work, even though it be only a little bush chapel by the wayside, or the sign of the cross above the doorway of someone's house.

Even secular historians have found themselves compelled, perhaps unwillingly, to pay attention to this strange phenomenon. It used to be the custom to pass it by in decorous silence as having no interest for the historian. In the four-teen volumes of the *Cambridge Modern History* which appeared in the early years of this century, there is only one reference to Christian missions and that purely fortuitously in connection with the journeys of the great David Living-stone who happened to be a missionary as well as an explorer. The *New Cambridge Modern History,* which is now in the process of appearing, does devote quite a lot of space to the missions, especially in its chapters on China and Africa, but on the whole the writers seem to regard the missions with irritation, as interlopers disturbing and dis-torting the natural course of historical development.

In quite recent times two notable changes have taken place. Supporters of Christian missions are looking back on their own history far more critically than they have ever done before, rewriting much of it in terms of independent and scholarly research. And secular historians, who have no vested interest in the matter at all, are beginning to recognize that the missions have been among the great creative forces that have brought new nations into being all over the world. It was a secular historian from Princeton who not long ago published a book with the title *Christian Missionaries and the Creation of Northern Rhodesia 1880–1924*.[1] Not everyone agrees with everything that was written in this book; the fact that it was written is what is important. Another writer, whose work gives evidence of little sympathy with the missionaries, writes at the end of a general survey of Africa that, at a time when governments, traders, and the missions themselves were cooperating to create a cultural vacuum in Africa, the missionaries and they alone were looking ahead and putting into the hands of Africans the instruments that would enable them, when the time came, to create afresh.[2]

We need not then apologize for inviting the reader to consider a theme which is so widely recognized to be significant.

It may be wise, however, to start by considering some objections to Christian missions which are commonly raised at the present time. At the beginning of this century it was generally accepted among practicing Christians that the command to preach the Gospel to every creature came directly from the Lord Jesus himself, that this obligation rests permanently on the Church, and that to become a "foreign missionary" is the highest form of self-dedication

1. Robert I. Rotberg, *Christian Missionaries and the Creation of Northern Rhodesia 1880–1924* (Princeton, New Jersey: Princeton University Press, 1965).
2. Paul Bohannan, *African Outline* (Harmondsworth, 1966), p. 216: "It was only the missions that began to rebuild and gave them a chance to rebuild."

open to a young man or woman. Today the attitude and atmosphere have notably changed. There are, no doubt, circles in which the old belief in the sacred right of Christians to put missions into operation whenever and wherever they can still lingers on. But many feel the subject to be an uncomfortable one, to be avoided if possible, to be at best hesitantly and tentatively discussed. The difficulties group themselves in three distinct settings.

There is the problem for the man who profoundly believes in the principle of religious toleration and of a pluralistic society. Christians have learned slowly and painfully that they have to be prepared to live peacefully alongside fellow citizens of other allegiances and commitments. The peoples of most Western countries have decided to try the great new experiment of complete religious toleration. Every man must be free to observe the tenets of any religion or of no religion as his conscience directs him; no man must suffer any diminution of civic right or privilege because he happens to adhere to one religion rather than to another. Catholics, Prostestants, and Jews (with the Orthodox regarded as perhaps a fourth distinctive community) have to live together in harmony and amity.

If this happy state of affairs is to be attained and to continue, the principle of noninterference with the religion of others must be strictly observed. Everyone knows how bitterly the Jews resent the attempts of Christians to convert them. Therefore, let the Christian keep to his own way, but let him leave to the Jew the freedom to find the God of his fathers in the way that his fathers have always found Him. But, if we are to keep to this principle in the West, should we not refrain from interference with the religion of the Hindus or the Japanese who live far way across the ocean and are much less immediately our concern?

The second difficulty is set forth by the cultural anthropologists and by those who have come under their influence.

The central thesis of many of these teachers is that each religion is integral to the culture of which it forms a part. A society needs cement to hold it together. This cement is provided by ideas and ideals which go a little beyond the needs of every day. Just because these ideas lie outside our ordinary experience, they will often find mythological expression and may be all the better for that. Myth is not sheer invention; it is a poetic or symbolic way of expressing something that is strongly held or that springs from the deepest experiences of the group or tribe. Such myths often find expression in sacred drama or in liturgical ritual. When this happens we have all the elements of religion. The more primitive the society, the clearer this becomes. An astonishingly large part of the time of such simple peoples as the aborigines of Australia is spent in liturgical practices. The very life of the tribe is held to be dependent on the correct performance of these ceremonies; without them the life of the tribe would simply fall apart.

It is for this reason, says the cultural anthropologist, that it is wrong to attempt to change any man's religion. All things hold together in the life of a society; each part is in subtle ways affected by every other part. If the religion is changed or undermined, the society as a whole will fall in pieces; its existence as a society has been destroyed. It is for this reason that, when missionaries have interfered with the life of simple peoples and have tried to change their convictions, these peoples have found themselves deprived of their reason for existence and in many places have simply begun to die out.

The third doubt or question comes from the side of young people conscious of the weaknesses and failures of Western civilization. We have made a tragic mess of things. We have failed to solve our problems. Twice in one century we have plunged the whole world into war and drawn millions of Asians and Africans into quarrels which were not their own. Have we any right to treat our culture as an article of export and to attempt to impose it on people who have no use for it? Would we not do better to attend to our own affairs and let other people attend to theirs?

All these questions or criticisms are formidable and must be faced by any who would defend the cause of Christian missions. The defense must be honest, relevant, and effective. What are the arguments that can be adduced on the other side?

One argument, of which a great deal was heard fifty years ago but which is hardly likely to be mentioned today, was to the effect that it was the Gospel which had made the Western nations strong and great, and therefore other nations that wished to emulate the West should also pay attention to the Gospel. It is interesting to see what that argument looks like from the other side. When the World's Parliament of Religions was held in Chicago in 1893, the speaker who probably made a deeper impression than any other was a young Bengali, Swāmi Vivekānanda. This is what he had to say about the kind of Christian propaganda which he had heard in India:

> All those that come over here from Christian lands to preach have that one antiquated foolishness of an argument that the Christians are powerful and rich and the Hindus are not, ergo Christianity is better than Hinduism, to which the Hindu very aptly retorts, that that is why Hinduism is a religion and Christianity is not; because, in this beastly world, it is Blackguardism and that alone that *prospers;* virtue always suffers. It seems however advanced the western nations are in scientific culture, they are mere babies in metaphysical and spiritual education.[3]

So the less heard of that argument the better.

3. *Life of Swāmi Vivekānanda,* 5th impression (Calcutta: Advaita Ashrama, 1955), pp. 514–5.

Another and even worse argument was sometimes addressed to doubters in the West whose interest it was hoped to engage for the cause—missions are good for trade; therefore support missions. Unfortunately this argument found its way into the columns of the *Encyclopedia of Missions,* which was published in New York in 1891. This old book is hardly known in the Western world today, but apparently it has been diligently studied by Christians in Communist China. The old bad argument has been disinterred from its resting place and used by these Chinese Christians in support of their contention that all Western missionary work in China was simply one manifestation of imperialistic aggressiveness, and that the missionaries themselves were so fatally compromised by their association with the policies of their capitalist governments that, when a revolutionary government took over, the only thing that it could possibly do was to get rid of them.

A rather more respectable argument runs as follows: the newly independent nations of the world have opted for democracy, and the form of democracy which they seem to wish to follow is that of Britain and the United States. But our democracy is a part of our Christian inheritance; it is derived not from certain general philosophical doctrines of the rights of man (as French democracy largely is) but from a belief in the equality of all men in the sight of their Creator and in the responsibility of all for each and each for all. If, then, these new states are to make a success of democracy, they must understand the Christian principles on which democracy is based. Where else will they learn, unless we set to work to teach them? This argument is at least respectable; it can claim to be based on a genuine interest in the peoples of the developing countries and on a desire to help them in other than material ways. I think, however, that it is in reality putting the cart

7

before the horse. It may well be that, if the peoples of Africa become Christians in larger numbers, they will improve their chances of political stability and progress. But the danger is that we may make the gospel a *means* to something else, and that is exactly what cannot be done. We are called always to be servants of the gospel; the gospel itself must always be master and not servant.

Let us try again. In the opinion of many church elders and treasurers far too much money goes out of Christian to non-Christian countries. They wonder how the missionaries manage to spend it all and where it all goes. The answer lies ready to hand: it really is not difficult to defend Christian missions on humanitarian grounds and in the light of the immense charitable work that they have carried on. Again and again people say, "Why do the missionaries not do this or that?" To which we may readily answer, "That is exactly what they have been doing for the last hundred years." In one field after another it was the missions which were the pioneers in service to the people. In the small part of South India which I know well the missions opened the first hospitals for women and children, the first schools for girls, the first asylums for lepers, the first schools for the blind and for the deaf. The government followed on long afterwards in all these fields.

But still we have not found our answer. A time may come when governments have taken over responsibility for every social need—for health, education, and the care of the young and the old—as it is maintained that they have done in Russia. The happy time may come when there will be no more poor, because all will have enough of all the good things of life. Does that mean that the work of Christian missions should automatically come to an end, because there will then be nothing left for them to do? If charitable activity was the sole concern of Christian missions, that would be the clear and logical conclusion. We must go still further and ask whether there is some factor of which we still have not taken account.

In the various arguments against missions and the various defenses of them, there is one question that has not yet been raised—the question of *truth*. If each religion is relevant merely to a particular culture, as the consecration of that culture by mythological reference, then the question of truth is already answered: religion of one kind or another may claim to be relevant or useful, as being the cement which holds society together, but it cannot establish any claim to be objectively *true* in the sense in which physics, chemistry, and other forms of knowledge based on actual observation of tangible realities are true.

The question of *truth* must be raised, but will it be possible to find any answer? How is the claim that one religion is true, or at least more true than another, to be reconciled with our principle of tolerance and of the plural society? If we affirm that Christianity is true, are we not bound to give mortal offense to our Jewish friend who lives by the truth that he has found and is not prepared to see it criticized in the light of another truth which is alleged by someone else to be superior? We can only reply that, whereas there should hardly be any limits to our tolerance of people as people, the moment we raise the question of truth, we are faced by the painful issue of the intolerance of truth. In this strange world of ours if one statement is true, any other statement inconsistent with it is necessarily untrue, or at least wide of the truth. If two and two make four, as they do in the arithmetic books but not apparently in the higher mathematics, then they cannot make three or five. If water is made up of two molecules of hydrogen and one of oxygen, then plain ordinary water cannot be produced in any other way.

9

This is self-evident in mathematics or physical science. But we do in fact apply this principle of contradiction in a great many other ways. We fought World War II on the principle that the Western way of life is the embodiment of certain great *truths* about the nature of man and about the way in which man ought to live in society, and that the Nazi way of life was an embodiment of such disastrous errors that the two views could not both be allowed to exist on the face of the earth. The democratic way of life, we think, tends to make real human beings in a free world; the Nazi system was bound to make men into machines operating in a slave world. It is fashionable nowadays to suggest that wars are never fought on principles but only in defense of material interests, perhaps happily disguised under great moral affirmations. All that can be said by those who are old enough to remember the crisis which fell upon Britain in 1939 and on the United States in 1941 after Pearl Harbor is that at the time it did not feel at all like that. One of the things that makes us human is the willingness to die for a cause that we see to be greater than ourselves and the defense of which we understand to be more important than our individual survival. But this means that we are making an affirmation of *truth*—certain things are true for all men and at all times. To contract out, to say, "That is no business of mine," is treachery to the whole human race.

So far so good. But when it is suggested that we carry the same principles into the field of religion, many people begin to be disturbed and unhappy. Yet, if we are to take religion seriously, is there any way by which the question can be evaded? The only reason for being a Christian is the overpowering conviction that the Christian faith is true.

What does it mean when we say that a religion is true? It means at least this—that the teachings of this religion are congruent at every point with everything that can be known, by other methods and from other sources, of this universe in which we live and of the life of man upon it, that answers can here be found to questions which have proved unanswerable by any other method, and that no future discovery of truth in other fields will be found to contradict the affirmations of this religion, though new light in other fields is likely to lead to fresh religious insights and to the modification of ancient formulations.

What then does it mean to be a Christian? With his usual skill in going to the heart of any matter with which he deals, Saint Paul puts it for us clearly and succinctly in the fifth chapter of his second letter to the Corinthians:

> Therefore, knowing the fear of the Lord, we persuade men . . . for the love of Christ controls us, because we are convinced that one has died for all; therefore all have died. And he died for all, that those who live might live no longer for themselves but for him who for their sakes died and was raised.

Here are no high and fine philosophical ideas, no complicated dogmas, but a number of plain statements. First, we are confronted with two statements of what is believed to be historical fact, that Christ died and was raised again from the dead. Then we are given a hint as to the interpretation of the fact—that in this death the whole of humanity was in some way involved. Third, there follows the claim that if this is true, the whole of the life of man has been changed, since from now on its focal point is to be not in man himself but in the Lord Christ.

But from the acceptance of this as truth there follows a further consequence—if all men are really concerned in these historic events, if all in some way are affected by the mysterious change that has taken place, they ought at least to be told about it. Hence, the obligation resting on the apostle and upon all other Christians to "persuade men," to tell them what has happened, and to plead with them to enter into the new possibilities that lie open to them, since in the resurrection of Jesus Christ the new creation is already here. To be a Christian means to be an ambassador.

The claim that the Gospel of Jesus Christ is the religion for all men is present in the witness of the Church from the very beginning. Luke puts it dramatically for us in his story of what happened on the Day of Pentecost when the Holy Spirit came down upon the waiting disciples. Jerusalem was crowded with pilgrims from many parts of the world and from many countries. There were Parthians, Medes, and Elamites and so on and so on. If we look at this list carefully, we shall see that Luke has made it representative of the three great families into which the Jews believed the human race to be divided. All are supposed to have sprung from the three sons of Noah—Shem, Ham, and Japheth. The mind of the early readers of the Acts of the Apostles would go back to another list of nations, that given in Genesis 10, where the nations are specifically grouped under these three headings. Most of the peoples mentioned by Luke fall under the heading of the Semites, Elam being the first of the Semitic nations mentioned in Genesis 10; but Luke is careful also to add Egypt and Libya which come under the heading of the Hamites, and Cretans (Kittim) and dwellers in Rome who belong to the section under Japheth. Luke does not draw attention to what he is doing; but in his own subtle way he is saying to us that on that day of Pentecost the whole world was there in the representatives of the various nations; the whole world was able to hear the message of "the mighty works of God," and everyone was able to understand.

12

In the last book of the Bible, the Revelation of Saint John, we are given a picture of "a great multitude which no man could number, from every nation, from all tribes and peoples and tongues, standing before the throne and before the Lamb" (Rev. 7:9). All the nations are to walk in the light of the city of God, and the glory and honor of the nations are to be brought into it (Rev. 21:24–5). It is not necessary to multiply the quotations—this sense that the Gospel is true for all men everywhere runs through the whole of the New Testament.

The earliest disciples were slow to realize all that was involved; they seem to have thought that they would stay in Jerusalem, still linked in many ways to the worship of the temple and of the old covenant, and that all the nations of the world would come up to Jerusalem, there to receive the Word of the Lord. Only when Jerusalem was destroyed by the Romans in A.D. 70 did the Christians finally realize that this expectation was not going to be fulfilled. Christianity, unlike Islam with its sacred city of Mecca, was never again to have one geographical center to which the eyes of all men would turn.

These early Christians may have been wrong as to the direction of the flow—it was to be outward from Jerusalem and not inward toward it. But concerning the central fact they were perfectly right—this Gospel must be made known to the nations. The Christian is "under obligation, both to Greeks and to barbarians, both to the wise and to the foolish," since he has come to understand that this Gospel "is the power of God for salvation to every one who has faith, to the Jew first and also to the Greek" (Romans 1:16–17).

Here, it must be granted, are a number of assumptions that modern man is not always ready to accept. Is it really possible to speak in this way of the whole of humanity

13

as a unity? We see diverse races, many different groups, countless civilizations and forms of society. Is there really any common history which unites us? Is not "human nature" an abstraction to which no reality corresponds? Christianity suits us in the West because we have grown up with it, our society has been deeply penetrated by its principles, and our minds have been conditioned from the cradle to receive it as revelation from God. But is this true of other races? Are not their minds so different from ours that what is evident to us must be unintelligible to them? If they were to accept the Christian faith, would they not make of it something so entirely different that in the end it would not be the same religion?

For the old-time believer in every word of the Bible the matter was, of course, quite simple. Adam and Eve were created by God, and all human beings are descended from them; therefore, the unity of the human race is a given fact. Today ethnologists would be less confident. When and how the creature called *homo sapiens* came into existence we cannot say. It may have been in one region only, but the majority of scientists would be prepared to reckon with at least the possibility that human beings appeared independently in various regions of the earth's surface. Yet it is quite clear that today we are all members of a single race.

It is possible for men and women of the most diverse races to copulate and produce healthy offspring. No doubt this mixing of races has been going on for a very long time; racial purity as imagined by the Nazis in Hitler's Germany is a myth—no such thing exists, and we are all certainly much more of a mixture than we imagine.

There is no language on earth which cannot be learned by those who do not naturally speak it. Some languages are more difficult to learn than others. But the nature of communication is everywhere the same; and, though the various structures of language represent different psychological approaches to reality, the difference is never so great as to produce a barrier which cannot be crossed from both sides. Even when a language has not been learned, a considerable measure of communication is possible by signs and even by the expression of the face. The minds of men and women work in much the same way all over the world. Misunderstandings are, of course, possible; but so they are between those who speak the same language—the cynic was not speaking wholly without reason when he said that words were given to us in order to conceal our thoughts.

There was a time when certain races could live in total separation from all the rest of the world. The Australian aborigines had been hidden away for many centuries from the eyes of all other men, with highly developed cultures of their own and with the utmost ingenuity in keeping themselves alive under conditions which others would find quite intolerable, yet at the same time without knowledge of even the simplest forms of agriculture. But those days are gone forever. Western man has poked his inquisitive nose into every corner of the earth, and the Australian aborigine no longer even looks up as the aircraft passes over his remote and peaceful dwelling. We are all now part of one family, and none of us can remain unaffected by what happens to another member of the family.

These are the facts. How are we as Christians to understand the facts? Is it true that God governs the nations of the world and mysteriously guides their history in accordance with purposes of his own? At the time at which the Gospel first appeared, the Roman Empire had brought to a great part of the ancient world a peace and a prosperity that had never been known before. The Gospel could be preached in a language, Greek, that was understood by educated men everywhere, from the mountains of Afghanistan to Marseilles and western Spain. Was this just chance? Or had God something to do with it? Is it just chance that we live in a world which, for good or ill, is unified as it has never been before? Or is the God who revealed himself in Jesus Christ making it plain to us as Christians that he is interested in all the nations of the earth, and that this new unity is part of his plan for them all?

If we take the Bible seriously, we see that from the beginning God has been interested in all the nations of the world, in the human race as a whole. Those first eleven chapters of Genesis, to which we have already referred, give us the background to the whole of the biblical revelation. It is God who has made man in his own image, as an intelligent creature who can seek after God and find him, as a being that can ponder and can worship. But man is also a rebellious creature who can demand an independence from God for which he was not made and can set his own will up in opposition to the will of his Creator. When, because of this human arrogance, the nations of the world have been scattered and each nation begins to speak its own separate language (Genesis 11), the way home to unity will be long, perplexing, and arduous.

With Genesis 12 a tremendous change takes place. From now on the plan of God is to go forward through one people and one national history. God will speak with the Jews as he does not speak with any other people. The story of the Old Testament is, in consequence, a story of contraction. The plan of God seems to work itself out on an ever narrower stage. Of the twelve tribes of Israel only two survive into later history. Of those out of the two tribes who were carried away captive into Babylon, only a small number came back to their own land. It was in this small and reduced community that Jesus Christ was born. In him the plan reaches its narrowest form, its moment of most intense concentration. At the crisis of his death he is "the man," the whole human race; on his perfect obedience to the Father the whole destiny of man, the fulfillment of the Father's plan of redemption, depends. That is why the death of Jesus Christ is the central event in the whole history of the human race.

But from this moment the plan once again begins to expand. We come back to Pentecost. The whole world is there in its representatives. The Gospel is now to be made available to all the nations. The time has come for all the nations to become part of the plan of God, to be gathered together into his kingdom.

This is, in fact, what has been happening over nineteen centuries. Professor K. S. Latourette in his seven volumes on *The Expansion of Christianity* has shown us that advance has not been continuous; there have been tremendous set-backs and losses, but retreat has always been followed by advance; the Christian Gospel has been like an incoming tide, spreading itself irresistibly across the wide beaches of the world. It is true that much in this process is mysterious to us. Why should one nation have been brought into the plan and not another? Why did Ireland become Christian earlier than England? Why did the Gospel come so late to Germany and later still to Scandinavia? Why did Christianity almost wholly die out in Asia where it had its origin?

It is easier to ask such questions than to answer them. God shows us certain things and bids us leave other things to his wisdom. But, at this point, there are three aspects of his mysterious working of which we do well to take note.

1) If we look back again to the Old Testament, we shall be reminded that God has not forgotten the nations of the world, even when they have not been brought directly into his plan. He has one *kairos* (appointed time) for one nation and another for another nation. But what student of the Chinese language, having observed the extraordinary beauty

and ingenuity of the characters in which it is written, could think that God had nothing to do with all this?

2) On every level of being of which we are aware, we find that it is God's method to go forward slowly from the very small to the very large. Where and when did life first appear upon the earth? We do not know. But we may accept the view of most scientists that, when it did appear, it was in the tiniest, frailest, and most vulnerable form that we can imagine. This first living thing was exposed to all the terrors of wind and storm, of fire and earthquake. How easily could it have been finally and irreparably extinguished! And yet life has survived and taken hold in land and sea alike. When this strange creature, man, made his appearance in the world, he was the feeblest of all beings. The human baby can do less to care for itself than the young of any other known creature. How easily could man have fallen a victim to the tooth of the tiger or the paw of the bear! But man was not annihilated. He has shown astonishing inventiveness in adapting himself to all kinds of situations and to every possible variation of climate, so that he can now exist in comfort in the heat of the Sahara or amid the frigidities of the South Pole.

It is not, then, in the least surprising that the new humanity in Jesus Christ came into the world under the guise of a frightened and anxious group of despised Jews in a minor city of a subprovince of the Roman Empire. How easily this little "church," as it learned to call itself, could have disintegrated through doubt about the reality of the Resurrection or through inner disputes and disagreements! How easily could it have been blotted out through Jewish or Roman persecution! But the church survived and grew; it has gradually extended itself throughout the inhabited earth, until in our day there is hardly a country in the world in which Christians are not to be found.

3) But why should God act so slowly and so partially? Why should he reveal himself to the Jews and not to any other nation in the same way? If God wished to reveal himself, should he not have revealed himself equally to all men everywhere and at the same time? Certainly it would have been possible for God to act in this way, and perhaps he has other worlds in which he has revealed himself in one single great act. But in no area of human life has he done so; here he has made himself dependent on human response and human intelligence. We may think that it is not contrary to the will of God that we have the comfort that we now enjoy. If we believe in God at all, we accept the fact that God put all these riches into the world for man's advantage, but he left it to man to use the intelligence that had been given to him and to find out all these things for himself. It is astonishing to recall that as recently as 1837 Faraday made the fundamental discovery on which all our modern use of electrical power depends, though the Greeks had carried out the first practical observations in this field two thousand years before his time. There are many parts of the world to which the benefits of Faraday's discoveries have not as yet been applied. Is it beyond belief that what is true in science is true also in religion? God will not compel any man to believe in Jesus Christ; our spiritual freedom is most carefully preserved. Is it surprising that we have not yet worked out all the implications of his message, and that there are many parts of the world in which the gospel has not yet been heard?

In this new situation, what is the relationship between the Christian churches and those parts of the world that are not yet Christian? One of the most encouraging features in the present-day world is the new sense of responsibility among the more prosperous nations—and that means almost exclusively the nominally Christian nations—for the less prosperous parts of the world. One result of the unification of the world has been that we have not been able to hide from our eyes the glaring disparity between the standard of living which we regard as natural for ourselves and the level on which the great majority of people is condemned to live. A strong humanitarian sense compels us to recognize that we are bound to help. A strong Christian sense makes it plain that this is part of our Christian duty.

We are all aware of the difficulties attendant on such giving from the West to the East. Much of the money has found its way into the wrong pockets and has never reached those for whose service it was given. Many young nations have squandered large sums on ill-planned projects which never had the smallest chance of attaining to success. If we help too much or in the wrong way, we may weaken and not strengthen the people we are trying to help; we may paralyze and not stimulate their capacity to help themselves. An impulsive and uncalculated generosity may frustrate the very purpose which was in the minds of the givers.

Yet, when all this has been said, the need is there, and the impulse to share is still there. If we have given in bad ways in the past, we must learn to give in better ways. If we have given without due thought, we must think again and find means by which our giving will really help and not weaken the recipients. We know that, as the rich and prosperous, we are under obligation.

But what is it that we are prepared to give? If famine threatens, we must send emergency shipments of grain to keep people alive. We must help to build hospitals and schools. If an American child falls sick, it will get the best possible attention. Penicillin and aureomycin and the other wonder drugs of the modern world have taken a great deal of the terror out of sickness and have greatly increased our expectation of life. But, if for the American child, why not also for the Korean orphan, and for the Congolese, and the Amazonian Indian? Have we any more right to these things than they? Do not their parents love them just as we love our children? The moment the question is put, it can be answered in only one way. We have and they have not. "If anyone has the world's goods and sees his brother in need, yet closes his heart against him, how does God's love abide in him? Little children, let us not love in word or speech but in deed and in truth" (1 John 3:17–18).

Let us carry the argument one step further. Is that which is relevant in the area of the body and its needs relevant also in the realm of the spirit? We are prepared to give wheat and corn and powdered milk and penicillin and quinine. We are ready to give ourselves in personal service. Have we any right to withhold from others the knowledge of God in Jesus Christ?

This question cannot be answered theoretically or by lofty argument. The meaning of it can be seen only when it is put in personal form. What would life mean to you, if you ceased to believe in Jesus Christ? This is something that can happen as a result of intellectual questionings, or of psychoanalysis, or of some strange pressure of circumstances. Each must answer the question in his own way.

One may well be able to answer, "Well, I imagine life would go on very much as before. Of course I would resign my membership in the church. But I would go to the office every morning as usual, and play a round of golf on Saturday, and clean the car on Sunday, and take the kids to our lake cottage in the summer, and vote Republican as I always have. I don't think that it would make any other difference." If any reader who has followed me up to this point must honestly give this kind of answer, let him now shut the book. The rest of it is not for him.

Another man may answer, "I don't know how I would go on living. I have learned to say with Paul, 'For to me to live is Christ.' Jesus Christ has become the center of my being. I try to bring him into my daily work. My wife and I have honestly tried to help our children to see that he matters more to us than anything else in the world. If I ceased to believe in him, the light would have gone out in the sky. I think I would want just to lie down and die."

If it matters to me as much as this, is there any man in the world to whom it ought to matter less? If I could not live without Christ, can I lie down comfortably in my bed at night so long as there is one single person in the world who has not heard of him? They must have bread, and they must have healing, and they must have education, and they must have peace. Can I try to give them all these things, and withhold from them the thing that matters more than all the rest put together—the love of God in Jesus Christ?

In the past our attempts to share our religion may have been often misguided and harmful. We have tried to force our gospel on other people, and that we have no right to do, since God scrupulously honors our spiritual freedom and integrity. We have given the gospel with a kind of condescension from the height of Western superiority, and that the proud and sensitive races of the East have naturally found intolerable. We have tangled up the gospel with all kinds of irrelevances and have made it seem a part of that Western imperialism which Asia and Africa today are so passionately repudiating.

We have a great deal to unlearn and a great deal for which we have to ask forgiveness. But, if we have in the past given badly, that means that we must learn to give better; it does not mean that we should not give at all. If we have given foolishly, we must learn to give wisely.

If we have given arrogantly, we must learn humility—and that is very hard for Western men to learn. Above all, we must understand that we shall receive in return tenfold more from those to whom we have the great honor to be allowed to give. But, as we value our own souls, we may not cease from giving.

2

What the
Missionaries
Did Wrong

A man I knew at the University of Cambridge became a missionary in China. Some years later he wrote that "missionary work is much more difficult than is generally supposed." This is a beautiful example of Cambridge understatement. Christian missionary work is the most difficult thing in the world. It is surprising that it should ever have been attempted. It is surprising that it should have been attended by such a measure of success. And it is not at all surprising that an immense number of mistakes should have been made.

In early days the pioneer missionary arrived at a certain place, perhaps on a certain island, where he could not speak a word of the language, where the inhabitants might well be dangerous, and where the local customs were unknown to him and confusing. How did he set to work to bridge the gulf, to make contact with these strange people who might look on him at the start with wonder and alarm, a little later with dislike, and then after a further period with indifference? How did he try to bring home to them the message of the gospel?

It was not long before the missionary became aware of features in the life of the people which to him were shocking and which he felt must be changed at the earliest possible opportunity. One of the earliest fields to which Prostestant missionaries were sent was the beautiful island of Tahiti in the Pacific Ocean. The famous explorer Captain James Cook had spent some time in the islands in 1767. From his careful accounts it seemed to the Western world that at last the earthly paradise had been discovered. Here was a fertile land where a beautiful and gifted people lived simple lives, amply provided for by the bounty of nature which yielded all that men could need without any great demand for hard work, and without the cares and anxieties which press on civilized men.

There was much truth in this picture. But this was only one aspect of the life of the islands—there was a shadow side as well. One day the chief with whom Cook had become friendly invited him to be present at a human sacrifice which was to be offered in order to secure favorable auspices for a war in which he was about to engage with a neighboring tribe. Cook accepted the invitation and has left a minute and accurate description of the scene. He noted that there were forty-nine skulls of earlier victims in the place, many of them quite clearly from recent sacrifices. Then, to quote the summary provided by Alan Moorehead in his excellent book *The Fatal Impact,* he went on to speak of

> how the ceremony continued for two days; of the drum-ming and chanting, of the disembowelling of the pigs, of the burial of the unfortunate man [a middle-aged man of the lowest class who had been clubbed to death the day before], and of the boy who in moments of eerie silence screamed aloud, supposedly in imitation of the voice of God. Cook says it was by no means a reverent or awed crowd which stood and watched; from time to time they turned their backs and talked of other things. But he does convey a feeling of supernatural tenseness that was in the air, a kind of bated and trance-like communion with an

invisible power that was being invoked through the sacrifice.[1]

Strangest of all, the artist John Webber, who was on board Cook's ship *Resolution* and who was also present, drew the scene—surely the most unusual picture ever produced from life by a European artist.

Minor wars between the tribes were a constant occurrence in the islands. By modern standards they were perhaps not very terrible. A party of twenty to thirty young men would go out one night on a raid. Not more than two or three would be killed on each side. But the usual accompaniment of such raiding was cannibalism. If you had killed your enemy you then proceeded to eat him—and those who had taken part in such feasts assured their visitors that the flesh of man tastes better than that of any other animal whatsoever. We are told that one of the first missionaries to arrive in Fiji began his missionary career by gathering and burying the heads, hands, and feet of eighty victims who had been cooked and eaten.

In many areas the earliest contacts of the missionary were with the darker side of the life of the people. These things are done in the daylight and cannot be hidden. The reaction of the missionaries, natural if not commendable, was to conclude that these beautiful peoples had fallen wholly into the snare of the devil, and that everything, as it came under observation, was wholly evil.

It is not fair to blame the missionaries alone for this point of view. As converts began to come in, they tended to take the same attitude towards their own past. Only in very rare cases does a convert speak of his former religion as having in any way prepared him for the coming of the

1. Alan Moorehead, *The Fatal Impact: An Account of the Invasion of the South Pacific, 1767–1840* (New York: Harper and Row, 1966), p. 68.

gospel. To him it is a world of darkness in which he had fallen under the spell of an evil power. The gospel has come as the great deliverance from a past with which he never again wishes to have anything to do. As observers from outside, we may see in that old system many things which were beautiful and true. But, in point of fact, man always experiences life as a whole. The convert will answer, "You cannot take a bit here and a bit there and say that this is good and that is bad. Every part of the system is dependent on every other part. It is the system as a whole that is corrupt and evil." As he has lived under the system and we have not, it is very hard for us to contradict him. And so missionaries and converts together became iconoclasts; the kindest thing they could say about the past would be, "Down with it, down with it, even to the ground."

Looking back with the advantage of hindsight, we can see that there were many things that might better have been preserved. Yet the problem is never simple. One obvious question relates to the use of music. Why did the missionaries reject the local form of music and introduce insipid Western tunes which are the expression of an entirely different musical idiom? The same answer comes from almost every country in the world. When missionaries have tried to set Christian words to the old tunes, the converts have been horrified: "You have no idea of the suggestions conveyed to us by those tunes. They belong wholly to the old and evil world, and it is quite impossible for us to associate Christian words with them. Our grandchildren may be able to do so, when the old associations have come to be forgotten. But for us, please, Christian tunes for Christian words."

Almost without being aware of it the missionaries had created a vacuum in the minds of the people they had come to serve. But nature abhors a vacuum. Any society, if it is to hold together at all, must have customs and rules. As many of the old rules had gone by the board, new rules had to be invented. The missionaries tended to think that what was good for the West would be good also for the Eskimo and the Polynesian and tended to produce as nearly as possible a replica of the society in which they themselves had grown up.

They were shocked by what appeared to them to be the total sexual promiscuity permitted in the societies in the midst of which they had settled. In point of fact the promiscuity was very far from total; the latitude was far greater than that recognized until recently in Western societies, but certain relationships were guarded by a strong taboo, and any breach of the rules was visited with severe penalties. This was not at first realized, and it was perplexing to the missionaries that the structure of the family in other countries is so entirely different from what it is in the West.

One of the aims, then, was to bring sexual irregularity under control. The missionaries came early to the conclusion that the almost universal nakedness of the people among whom they lived was the cause of the problem, and that, if they could be persuaded to wear clothes, their unruly instincts would be made subject to a higher law. In this they were doubly wrong. India is a land in which clothes play a very important part in the life of society; yet it is also the country in which ritual prostitution at the temples flourished until the most recent times. In Patagonia in the extreme south of South America, the missionaries were distressed to see the people endure the bitter cold of winter with hardly any protection at all. They secured for them warm winter clothing, unaware that this was the worst thing they could possibly have done; the resistance of the people to the elements, built up over many generations, was weakened, and they fell victims to all kinds of diseases previously unknown.

The early missionaries, like other Westerners in the tropics, were on the whole conventional people. They took it for granted that, whatever the climate, they would continue to wear what they had worn at home. If in Britain the preacher wore a top hat and a long black coat, that is what he would wear in Timbuktu or Tahiti. John Pollock in his book, *Hudson Taylor and Maria,* tells an amusing story of the effect of this getup on a Chinese audience. The young Hudson Taylor had been preaching to a Chinese crowd in the open air and felt that for once the difficulties of the Chinese language had been sufficiently mastered for the interest of his hearers to be secured. One man in particular had kept his eyes fixed on the preacher. When the discourse was over, this man requested permission to ask a question. He had been able to understand why the learned preacher's long black coat had buttons down the front—these could be used to close the coat against wind or rain. But what in the world was the purpose of the three little buttons across the back? This, and this alone, was the question which had held his attention enthralled during the preaching of the gospel!

But the missionaries were not alone to blame. There were other white men in the islands. Christians, and others too, are imitative. To wear clothes became the sign of a "civilized" man; those who wished to become "civilized" took over the less desirable, as well as the better, elements of Western civilization. And, when churches began to grow up and elders and ministers to be ordained from among the local people, it became a point of honor and prestige that the indigenous minister should look as nearly as possible like his Western friend. If the missionary wore a top hat, the Fijian minister would wear a top hat. If European

Anglican clergy wear a black cassock, the African clergy-man will wear a black cassock too, though any other color looks better against the African skin. And this tradition can be turned against the venturous missionary who attempts to change it. When a young missionary in Ghana announced that he was not going to wear a long black coat to preach in, his congregation replied, "In that case you will not preach." He would not give way, and they would not give way; in consequence he never preached.

So clothes can have a deep symbolic significance. This is exactly what they had in the days of the great conflict between the Gospel and the old ways in the Pacific Islands. To go almost naked advertised your resistance to Christian teaching and your determination to retain at every point the teachings of the ancestors. To begin to wear clothes was the outward and visible sign of your willingness to become subject to Christ. James Paton, the son of the famous John G. Paton of the New Hebrides, gives an amusing account of an elderly lady whose resistance to the gospel had been vociferous and of long standing but who at last gave way and decided to become a Christian. The sign of her submission was that the following Sunday she came to church decked with every article of European clothing on which she had been able to lay her hands, including a pair of men's trousers which she had donned as a kind of stole around her neck. Those who have some idea of the enormous heroism involved in the good lady's decision will be more inclined to kiss her feet than to mock at her unawareness of the way in which European clothes should be worn.

Clothes catch the eye. They are only the outward sign of very much deeper problems. In many areas of the world a nascent church has been faced by the problem of polyg-amy. What is to be done about the man who has more wives than one and who yet wishes to become a Christian? Many Africans today defend the view that polygamy is the natural form of the African family, and that the church should adapt its rules and customs to that which is natural to Africa.

The missionaries held the view, which they had brought with them from an entirely different kind of society, that polygamy is in every circumstance wrong, that to be a Christian means to be monogamous, and that therefore a man who wishes to be baptized must put away all his wives except the first. This is the classic example of the perils involved in the transference of the principles of one society, without due consideration, to another society which has been developed on very different principles. What the missionaries should have done is a question that will be debated for a great many years to come; what we can see clearly today is that what they did was not what they should have done.

Almost without exception missionaries have worked on the principle that what is good for the West in matters of worship is good for everyone else as well. The Roman Catholic Church has had a good deal of experience with what are called the Uniate Churches, fragments of the ancient Eastern Churches which have associated themselves with Rome and have been allowed to keep their old liturgical language and some of their earlier customs, including in certain cases even the retention of a married clergy. But, with the single exception of that part of the ancient Church of the Thomas Christians in India which adheres to Rome, such concessions have not been granted to any church which has come into being in Asia or Africa or the South Seas as a result of the modern missionary movement. For a brief period it looked as though it might be otherwise. In the seventeenth century the Jesuit Fathers in China had translated the liturgical books into classical Chinese, and we do hear from time to time of Mass being said in Chinese. But this practice soon fell into disuse. With the reaction of the eighteenth century against all innovation, it was laid down that Mass must be celebrated in exactly the same way all over the world, except where some ancient permissions for small variations were held to be still in force. So African priests with a scanty knowledge of Latin had to say Mass in Latin for congregations which could not understand a word of it. No doubt the sense of mystery was enhanced, but understanding cannot be said to have been promoted. Not until after the Second Vatican Council was this situation changed.

In Protestant circles, though greater liberty prevailed, the missionaries on the whole continued to do just what they had always done at home. The Anglicans, wherever they were, set to work as soon as possible to translate the whole of the Book of Common Prayer, sometimes even before the translation of the New Testament was completed. The only part of the Prayer Book not translated into the languages of India was the "Form of Prayer for Use by Those at Sea"; and, seeing that the majority of Anglican Christians in India have never seen the sea, this was perhaps a comparatively innocuous omission.

Here, again, we must not too much blame the missionaries. We tend to forget the length of time that elapses between the arrival of the missionaries and the constitution of the first local congregations. In New Guinea the Lutheran missionaries reckoned that ten years were likely to pass before the first baptism in a new tribe, and that only after twenty years could anything like a congregation be counted on. During all these years the missionaries had been holding services for themselves in their own language—

singing the Lord's songs in a strange land [2] was sometimes almost the only consolation left to discouraged Christians when their neighbors just would not be converted. In tropical countries everything is done with open doors and windows. Naturally the non-Christians very soon got to know exactly how Christians worship. In one area they had seen the Anglican missionaries gather every evening round a table with a lighted candle on it, fall on their knees and bury their heads in their hands. Naturally the watchers supposed them to be calling up mighty spirits from the earth, and concluded that, if and when they became Christians, they would be able to do the same themselves and in exactly the same way.

The new Christian does not wish to be put on a lower level than his Western friends. If that is the way in which they worship, that is the way in which he too will worship. During the pioneer period he has come to know what Christian singing sounds like, and many of the tunes have become quite familiar to him. If Anglicans in England have thirty-nine Articles of Religion, the newly converted Anglican will not be put off with thirty-eight.[3]

All these things could not have been foreseen, but cumulatively they have tended to stamp a Western character on the younger churches. In nothing are we more conservative than the way in which we worship God and in which we say our prayers. If a younger church has been in existence for fifty years, it may be given all the freedom in the world, but the last thing that it is likely to do is to set to work radically to modify its liturgical order. And, even if it has been free from the start, it is almost certain

2. Psalm 137:4.
3. The Protestant Episcopal Church in the United States of America has only thirty-eight!

to look to the nearest model and to copy it exactly. Under the influence of the great Hendrik Kraemer the little group of Christians in Bali (Indonesia) was taught from the beginning to regard the church as its own and to exercise its liberty to make its own decisions. As a consequence the Balinese Church is as much like the Dutch Reformed Church in Holland as any other church brought into being by that country.

Worse, and more serious than almost anything else, was the way in which the Westerner came to exercise financial dominance over his less developed brother. Missionaries, until the most recent times, have been extremely poor in comparison with members of their own race who have adopted any other vocation or profession. As a missionary I was paid just one-tenth of that which was being earned by my University friends who had entered the service of the government; and, naturally, those engaged in commerce or industry were receiving a great deal more. The missionary society I served did not supply its missionaries with cars, so for twelve years I went about South India on my bicycle— an experience I do not in the least regret, though the fact is that when after a friend gave me a well-used car my health began immediately to improve.

But, live as near to the soil as he can, the Westerner always appears to the Indian villager or to the South Sea islander to be extremely rich. He brings with him the trappings of an industrialized civilization, and he understands the use of money. When the missionaries arrived in the South Seas a hundred and seventy years ago, metal of any kind was entirely unknown. The natives got on very well without it, and had all kinds of ingenious ways of doing things for which we should regard metal tools as indispensable. But Western contrivances save a great deal of time. The Tahitians very soon began to hanker after the things which the sailors had brought with them and incidentally to purloin them with extraordinary skill. To the charming maidens of the islands a single nail represented all that was desirable; and they were quite ready to use that commodity which lay most readily at their disposal to secure so precious a possession.

The missionaries ought to have foreseen the danger. But they were aware of the deep poverty and helplessness of the people, even in a land that supplied so plentifully all that was immediately necessary for food and clothing, and were anxious to be of service to them. It did not seem right to exact labor for nothing in such matters as the building of houses and later the erection of churches, though that was what in fact the local chiefs had always done. So it became the custom to give little presents to those who had worked—some small tool, a handful of nails, a comb, objects of little worth to the European giver but of untold value to the recipient. Inevitably a wrong relationship came to be established. The local inhabitant came to look on the missionary as a good milk cow from whom the last drop of milk was to be extracted by any method whatsoever; the missionary came unconsciously to take up a patronizing or proprietary attitude towards those who had come to be dependent on his bounty.

Until very recently money was hardly used at all in an Indian or Chinese village. The village washerman and barber knew that at harvesttime they would be entitled to a certain share of the grain that had been gathered. Even the village schoolmaster was kept going by gifts in kind according to an established tariff, supplemented by extra gifts from boys whose parents had reasons for wishing to keep on the right side of the teacher. The missions long ago introduced a money payment for their catechists and teachers. The amount might be very small, but it at once disrupted the economy of the village; in a moneyless land the man who has even a little money in his pocket is a king—a very dangerous situation when the money is foreign money, and the recipient is almost bound to be regarded as having become the servant of a foreign power.

Missionaries in early days tended to exaggerate the poverty of their people and to underestimate their capacity to give. It is true that from about 1851 onward the great missionary thinkers, Henry Venn in England and Rufus Anderson in America, had begun to put forward the idea of self-governing, *self-supporting,* and self-propagating churches. But this tended to be regarded as an ideal for a rather distant future. What was lacking was biblical, thoughtful, systematic teaching on Christian stewardship, as a result of which new Christians from the start would have been led to realize that the church was their church, for which from the start they must be ready to take their share of responsibility.

Inevitably, Christians from the Western world brought with them their own divisions. It is impossible for any one of us to be "just a Christian," in the same way that it is impossible to be "just a human being." We have to be citizens of one state or country, and, if we are so minded, to use that as the starting-point for fulfilling our international obligations. In the same way we have to belong to one or the other of the Christian denominations, if we are to serve the worldwide and ecumenical cause of Christ. Those who have tried to live otherwise and to set themselves free from denominationalism have almost always ended by forming a new denomination. Missionary societies which have started off as "undenominational" have almost in every case found themselves before long serving as the mission of one denomination. The London Missionary Society was founded in 1795 on interdenominational lines but before long came to serve in practice as the missionary organ of the Congregational body in England.

Most missionaries have gone out into the non-Christian world flaunting the flag of this or that denomination, bearing names which are practically untranslatable into any other language and in any case could have no meaning for those who had grown up in circumstances very different from those which had led to the formation of this or that particular denomination.

In point of fact Christian divisions have wrought less harm than might have been expected. Both Hinduism and Islam are themselves religions of many sects—traditionally it is said that there are seventy-two sects in Islam, though I am not sure that anyone has succeeded in enumerating them all. No Hindu or Muslim is therefore greatly surprised if Christians find themselves in different groupings; the basic fact that these are Christians is recognized by all. Each tribe in Africa, each caste in India, has its own gods; it is not surprising if something like tribal forms of Christianity have emerged. In the days of the great mass movements in the Telugu area of South India, the great success of the Anglicans was with the Mala caste, that of the Baptists with the Madigas. The Anglican was known as the Mala-missionary, the Baptist as the Madiga-missionary. It might well happen that in a single village there was a church of each denomination. This caused little confusion, since the two castes carried on their separate existence as before, with the sole difference that both were now Christians though members of different Christian groups.

Nevertheless, the harm wrought to the cause of Christ by Western divisions has been very great. It is not difficult to understand the furious protest of an Indian convert against the system in which he felt himself to have been caught up: "The missionaries say that they have come to India just to preach Christ. All that they really want is to get people into their own little cages—and when they have got them there, they will not even allow them to receive the Holy Communion together."

It has been difficult for Christian missionaries to avoid becoming involved in political affairs which have nothing to do with the gospel. In precolonial days everything depended on the will of the local chief or sovereign. Without his permission and approval the missionary could not exist or settle. It was natural that he should set himself to keep on the right side of the chief. The chiefs also soon saw that it could be of use to them to have at their courts a tame missionary or two to help them in carrying on correspondence with the European powers or in mediating between their subjects and the troublesome Europeans—traders, hunters, and so on—who had settled inconveniently near their borders. Often this worked very well. The services of the wise French and Swiss missionaries to the great chief Moshoeshoe I (d. March 11, 1870), as he created what is now the independent country of Lesotho, were of incalculable value. The extreme case was that of Christian Friedrich Schwartz (in India 1750–98), greatest of all Protestant missionaries in South India, who for some years was actually prime minister of the small independent kingdom of Tanjore and guardian of the young heir to its throne. There is no evidence that Schwartz ever made use of his position for ulterior motives, but inevitably something of his personal prestige rubbed off on the Christian cause which he represented.

The problem was great, though not insoluble, when there

was only one chief. What was to happen if a country was divided between a number of warring chieftains? This was the situation in many of the Pacific islands. The missionaries without knowing it had been drawn as pawns into the infinitely complicated moves and counter-moves of local politics. Having committed themselves to friendship with one chief whose authority they in many cases imagined to be much greater than it actually was, they found themselves playing his game, to the detriment of their influence in all the areas not directly under his control. Disaster was added to difficulty when the rival chiefs managed to secure the support of rival missions. This was the situation in Samoa. The London Missionary Society had long been at work and had converted large sections of the population, when the Roman Catholics came in and started their mission. A disputed succession to the kingship found the missions on opposite sides. The situation was becoming so painful and dangerous that all parties were relieved when the Germans cut the Gordian knot by occupying the islands and declaring Samoa to be a German colony (1900).

The majority of the missionaries in early days lived far beyond the limits of the territories occupied by the colonial powers. They neither had nor asked for military or consular protection. If they were killed, the survivors sorrowed over them but made no demand for retribution or reprisals. When in 1839 the great pioneer in the South Seas, John Williams, was killed and eaten by the inhabitants of the island of Erromanga, no expedition was sent to take vengeance or to extort compensation from those who had done the wrong. A ship of war was, indeed, dispatched to the island to recover the bodies or all that was left of them; but the Governor of New South Wales, Sir George Gipps, would not agree to the dispatch of the vessel until he had wisely satisfied himself "that no revengeful purpose had prompted" the request.[4]

Nevertheless, the servant of Christ does not cease to be a member of a particular race and a citizen of one country. He believes that the institutions of his own country are the best, and that other peoples can only be benefited by the introduction of these institutions. The French, in particular, have an unshakable belief in the value of French culture. When the great Cardinal Lavigerie (1825–92), Archbishop of Algiers, was sending out his White Fathers into the undiscovered depths of Africa, he said to them, *Nous travaillons aussi pour la France*—"We are working for France [as well as for the kingdom of God]." The British are not far behind the French in their conviction that the British way of doing things is always the best. When the missionaries won positions of influence in the Pacific islands, one of their first thoughts was to replace what seemed to them the chaotic disorder of native justice, or injustice, by something remarkably like the British system of trial by jury. It is not unknown for Americans to suppose that the American way of life is something earnestly desired by those who have it not.

There is, however, a vast gulf between belief in a particular kind of civilization as something that readily goes together with the dissemination of the gospel and the desire that independent countries or islands should actually be taken over and ruled by one's own government. To such advance of colonial control missions have on the whole been resolutely opposed. Having seen all too much of the harmful effects of the contacts between the stronger and the weaker races, they feared the extension of such contacts that was

4. E. Prout, *Memoirs of the Life of the Rev. John Williams* (London, 1843), p. 585.

bound to result from the establishment of colonial government. Only in three situations do missionaries seem to have modified this attitude.

The first arose in the South Seas, when it became clear that the local powers could no longer control the situation. More and more white men, not always of the most desirable type, were coming in. The native races were threatened with disappearance as the result of the new weapons of war and the diseases which the white men had introduced. The kings and chiefs were powerless to prevent degeneration and disaster and themselves petitioned again and again that their islands should be taken over by some protecting power. It is hard to say that the missionaries were wrong at this point; the problem of the islands today is not the disappearance of simple and charming races but that of over-population! Under colonial rule the Polynesians and Melanesians have thrived and multiplied.

The second case arose when it became obvious that annexation was likely to occur, and missionaries became anxious that it should be their own nation and not any other which should profit by the opportunity. Eighty years ago it became clear that the kingdom of Buganda would hardly be able to maintain its independence. It was threatened by the extension of Arab power from the north. The German Carl Peters, one of the really aggressive imperialists of the nineteenth century, was engaged in making treaties with chiefs in all directions. The French and British missionaries were strongly entrenched at the court of the Kabaka, the local king, and could hardly dissociate themselves from political concerns. It was the unanimous wish of the British residents that Uganda should be taken under the protection of the British crown. This was what happened, and in 1894 the British protectorate was established.

The third situation was that brought about by slavery and the slave trade. Great Britain had outlawed the slave trade in 1807 and for two generations kept gunboats patrolling the whole of the west coast of Africa to make sure that the embargo was enforced. But the travels and discoveries of David Livingstone from 1854 till his death in 1873 revealed to the world that another terrible form of the slave trade was eating into the vitals of Africa from the east coast. The Arab traders were experienced, remorseless, and well-organized, and they were penetrating ever further into the interior. The one region which had up till that time been free from the horrors of the slave trade was the area later to be known as the Belgian Congo. But by 1882 the Arabs were firmly established on the headwaters of the Congo. It was clear that unless something was done, before many years had passed Arab slave raiders would extend their operations from the Arabian Sea to the Atlantic Ocean.

It was at this point that missionaries in Africa, almost to a man, became convinced that the only possible remedy for the evil was control by European powers. What they desired came about, though not in every case with consequences that they had foreseen. Belgium, Britain, and Germany took over the threatened areas, and slavery became an evil memory of the past.[5]

Once colonial occupation was a reality, even the missionaries who had been most opposed to it accepted the fact and settled down to make the new situation as acceptable as possible to the people among whom they worked. From the point of view of the new governments the mis-

5. It was finally abolished by the British in Tanganyika in 1922. There can be no doubt that slave trading still carries on a clandestine existence in Africa, though on a minute scale as compared with its ravages in the nineteenth century.

sionaries were the ideal allies. They had long lived among the people, and they knew the languages and understood the local customs. They, as no one else, could explain to the people what was happening and secure their unresisting acceptance of it. The alliance was profitable to both parties.

For a time all seemed to go extremely well. The missions could not but welcome the first and obvious fruits of colonial control—peace and order over large areas instead of internecine war, the suppression of slavery and cannibalism, and the improvement of communications which made it far easier to come and go. The new situation offered great opportunities for the development of the work. In the British territories the government was quite prepared to let the missionaries carry out the greater part of educational work, generously subsidizing all schools that would submit to government inspection and keep a number of simple rules. No hindrance at all was placed in the way of religious education in such schools. Even today about eighty percent of the schools in Tropical Africa are mission schools.

From many points of view this appeared to be a satisfactory situation. The government was able to get its educational work done more cheaply and more efficiently than had it done it itself. The missions were able to expand their work to an extent that would have been unthinkable without this government aid and were able to bring hundreds of thousands of young Africans under Christian influence. The people were well-satisfied. Africa was developing a passion for education, not so much from a disinterested love of knowledge as from the realization that education was the way to power, to acquiring that secret of the white man which made him strong and rich.

All went well as long as governments, peoples, and missions were getting along happily together. Many among the inhabitants of these countries were aware of, and grateful for, the benefits that came to them from colonial rule. What the ordinary man wants more than anything else is peace, and the certainty that a man who sows a crop will reap it. Where this security has long been lacking, there will for a time be a considerable measure of gratitude to those who have restored it.

But this state of patriarchal rule and grateful obedience could not continue forever. National movements and the desire for independence were bound to arise. When this came about the ambiguous position of the missions and churches immediately became clear.

It appeared to a great many nationalists that missions were so closely linked to governments as to have lost their independent status and to have abandoned their freedom to take up new attitudes corresponding to the new situation. Missionaries on the whole are conservative; it came to be widely taken for granted that they, and their national employees, would always be found on the side of the *status quo* and in opposition to what the nationalists affirmed to be the forces making for freedom and human dignity.

On behalf of the missionaries it must be said that the extent of their identification with the people whom they served has been much underestimated. Almost without exception they have remained at their posts, if allowed to do so, whatever political changes may have taken place. When India became independent in 1947, not a single missionary of any confession left the country in protest against the political revolution. In the Congo missionaries stayed on at posts of danger in the unhappy days of disorder, and about two hundred of them lost their lives. If they have been forcibly ejected, as from the Southern Sudan, they spend their time wondering when it will be possible for them to return to the land and to the people whom they love.

Yet, when all this has been said, it is still true that missions and churches have in many cases been out of step with the times. They have allowed themselves to become identified with a past that was already on the way out and so have prejudiced their chance of being accepted in a revolutionary and dynamic present. The colonial involvement of missions is as yet far from having been lived down.

The greatest mistake of all made by the missionaries has been that in many cases they stayed on too long and monopolized positions of authority and responsibility in the church. At the start the missionary had to be everything. Most of his converts were illiterate; he was the only educated Christian in the place and the source and fount of both knowledge and authority. If he worked in an out-of-the-way area, such as New Guinea or the Batak country in Sumatra, he had to be architect and builder, road surveyor, well digger, doctor and dentist, lawgiver and judge, and half a dozen other things besides. If the work was to be done at all, if houses were to be built, and streams to be bridged, and gardens to be cultivated, and children to be taught, his was the way in which it had to be done. Of course the greater part of the work was done by the "natives," but the missionary was the director; he gave the orders and expected to be obeyed.

Some of the early missionaries saw clearly that this could only be a temporary situation and that a missionary's job must be to work himself out of a job. At a very early date these wise prophets adopted measures to enable their converts to take independent action on their own. In the South Seas the London Mission did a heroic job of sending out teachers from one island group to another, as missionaries to people who in some cases were as foreign to them as they were to Europeans. Such teachers lived in complete isolation and sometimes under conditions of considerable danger; they could not possibly receive a visit from a missionary more than once a year. The worst among them were total failures; the best developed qualities of leadership, Christian character, and independence that fitted them to take their place with dignity in any Christian assembly. A rather similar method was used in the Lutheran missions in New Guinea, where evangelists who had received very little training were sent as pioneers to the unreached tribes.

This was excellent, but in reality the missionary was still in control. Even where he had called into existence an advisory council, the last word always remained with him and he controlled the money. At the end of the nineteenth century missionaries were clinging even more tightly to the control of the churches than earlier in the century. One reason for this was the disastrous results that followed upon some hasty and ill-considered attempts to transfer responsibility from the hands of the missionaries to the younger church that was coming into existence. In the area best known to me, from 1877 on all missionaries were withdrawn from pastoral work, and the entire responsibility was put into the hands of Indian clergy who had received little education and no training at all for the kind of work that they were now expected to do. Within a few years this rapidly growing church of sixty thousand people was in chaos. A new generation of missionaries came out to do evangelistic work among educated Hindus. Actually what they had to do was to spend thirty years of backbreaking work getting the church back into order. In the process they acquired a total distrust in the capacity of Indian Christians for responsible leadership. Hasty improvisation had set back by many years the cause of the independence of the Indian Church.

But even where there were no such special problems foreign control lasted far too long. Under the leadership of Ludwig Ingwer Nommensen (1834–1918), one of the greatest Protestant missionaries of all times, a wonderful movement came into being among the Batak people of Sumatra. By 1911 there were 103,525 Christians in the church. From an early date missionaries had educated Bataks to cooperate in the work of the church. From 1883 onwards pastors were trained and ordained. One church order succeeded another; nominally an independent church was coming into being. Yet in point of fact all control still rested in the hands of the missionaries who had developed an extraordinarily efficient system of supervision and direction. One who knew the situation well has told us that apparently Nommensen and his colleagues had never even imagined that these churches for which they had cared could one day exist without missionaries, and in separation from the mother church in Barmen (Germany).

The day came, during the Second World War, when the church had to exist without missionaries—all had been interned. The Bataks accepted the new situation with feelings of immense relief and deliverance. At last they were free to be themselves. At last they had a church which they could really call their own. To this day the third great festival of the church year, after Christmas and Easter, is that of the liberation of the Batak Church. From what was it liberated? Not from the old evil spirits, nor from the Dutch or the Japanese, but from the control of the missionaries!

3

What the Missionaries Did Right

Having come to the end of the last chapter, the layman may be inclined to throw down the book and to say: "I always thought this missionary business was phoney, and now by their own confession I know that it is so." It is indeed a damaging report that we have produced; we have tried to set down nothing in malice, but also nothing to extenuate. The missionary's standards for himself are high. If he fails to come up to his own high standards, he should be the first to recognize and to acknowledge the failure.

But perhaps there is also something to be said on the other side.

One of the advantages of knowing the language of a younger church really well is that one gradually comes to learn a number of things which are hidden from colleagues not so well equipped. Christians in these churches rarely talk to Westerners about missionaries and will hardly ever do so in a Western language. When one has come to know them well, they sometimes begin to open up, and the missionary gradually becomes aware of a new world. The "natives" have an endless store of anecdotes about missionaries, about their stumbling efforts to speak the language, and the many ludicrous mistakes in speech and action that they have made. These tales reveal a painfully acute and accurate assessment of all the foibles and weaknesses of the foreigner and precise acquaintance with what is supposed to be secret—missionaries like others forget that servants come to understand a great deal more English or French than they can speak, and that what is discussed at table or near an open window will be common property within a very short time.

If at the right moment one ventures to ask, "Tell me, what did you really think about the old missionaries?" the answer is likely to be something like this: "They were perfectly awful: arrogant, dictatorial, so sure that they were always right, arbitrary and capricious in their methods—but we did not mind all that too much, because we knew that they really loved us."

The great Thomas Gajetan Ragland, pioneer of itinerating evangelism in South India, died in 1858. More than forty years after his death a missionary asked a pastor who had been trained by him about Ragland's methods in the preparation of his students for the ministry. The old man thought for a few moments, and then said quietly, "He loved us. He loved us very much. Yes, very much he loved us."

It is the wise rule of almost all missionary societies that those who represent them abroad should retire at a certain age, and that, if they decide as many do to settle in the country where they have worked, they should not live in the actual district in which they served. So the time inevitably comes when the missionary has to pull up stakes, to leave the familiar scenes and the people who have become to him as his friends and his children. As that time approaches, many I think have heard the words of the prophet Jeremiah pronounced as a sentence of doom upon themselves: "To the land to which they will long to return, there they shall not return." [1] If this is more than

1. Jeremiah 22:27.

sentimental imagining, how have missionaries tried to give practical expression to the love that they have come to feel for their people?

The first thing, of course, was to get to know them, and the key to knowledge has always been the language. At least part of the Bible has now been printed in 1,392 languages. For more than 1,000 of these translations missionaries have been responsible. Perhaps nine-tenths of them have been carried out in languages which had never been written down until the missionaries took them in hand, made a script, and for the first time gave them written form.

To learn a language even with the help of grammar, dictionary, and existing literature is hard enough. To work on a language of which not a single word is known is almost unimaginably difficult. Those who have never *seen* words, as distinct from hearing them, hardly ever speak distinctly. Even when we have learned to ask the simple question, "What is that?" it is by no means certain that we shall get the answer that we expect. The inquirer meets a man carrying three fish and asks his question. The answer he gets may mean "three," or may be the general word for fish, or it may indicate the particular kind of fish that has been caught—or it could even mean "for my mother." Barbrooke Grubb, the pioneer among the Lengua people of the Paraguayan Chaco, reported that eleven years had passed before the missionaries felt themselves able readily to talk with the people and seventeen before they were able to baptize their first convert.

It is comparatively easy to draw up a list of words representing the things that can be seen and touched, and some of the more obvious verbs of action, such as "to cut" or "to sow." The difficulty is greatly increased when we begin to move into the realm of abstraction—and some abstract words are needed if we are ever to begin translation of the Scriptures. The story is told of a missionary in Africa who had sought long and without success for any word that would serve for "faith" in the New Testament sense of "trust" or "self-commitment." One day he was standing on a rather rickety ladder mending the roof of his house, when he heard one boy say to another: "If I were the missionary, I would not ——— that ladder." Was that the long-sought word? He hurled himself down the ladder, caught the boy, and demanded, "What was that you said?" The boy trembled, wondering what in the world he had done to make the white man angry. When with some difficulty it was made clear to him what was wanted, he did what we would all do in similar circumstances—repeated his remark in some entirely different form. Only after long coaxing was the missing word elicited from him, and it proved to be exactly the word which had been so long and vainly sought.

It was, however, not only in the completely unknown languages that the missionaries did the exhausting work of creating grammar, dictionary, and the beginnings of a literature. William Carey, the great Bible translator, performed the feat, unique for a foreigner, of laying the foundations of an entirely new kind of literature in the Bengali language. Bengali, a rich and musical form of speech, had a literature of its own when Carey was at work at the beginning of the nineteenth century; but this was all in a classical style, heavily larded with Sanskrit words, and as unintelligible to the ordinary reader as *Paradise Lost* is to the farmhand or the truck driver today. Carey's *Bengali Colloquies,* based on the ordinary speech of the people, are recognized by Indian scholars as having been one of the first steps in the direction of the flourishing Bengali prose literature of the present day.

The language is the first step. The second is to get to know the people behind the words. The first is hard; the second is even harder.

In many areas the missionaries were so shocked by what they found going on among the people as to have little desire to penetrate or to understand what they regarded simply as a kingdom of Satan. From the other side the people were not anxious to reveal their secrets—knowledge of a secret conveys power. In many cases they were themselves unable to give any explanation of why certain things were done—that was the way in which the ancestors had said things were to be done, and that is the way in which they always have been done, and so on world without end.

Almost from the start, however, there was another school of missionaries which held that if a missionary was to preach with any effect, he must understand the world into which he was speaking and the beliefs and ideas of his hearers, however strange or disagreeable these might be. The very first Lutheran missionary in India, Bartholomew Ziegenbalg (in Tranquebar 1706–19), produced two highly meritorious books, *The Genealogy of the Malabarian Gods* and *Malabaric Heathenism*. He sent his manuscript home to the headquarters of the mission at Halle. All he received was a sharp reminder that it was his business to preach the Gospel to the heathen in India and not to propagate heathen superstitions in Europe! His manuscripts lay forgotten in the archives of the mission for more than a century and a half, until *The Genealogy* was unearthed a hundred years ago by the distinguished missionary scholar, Wilhelm Germann, and so at last saw the light of day.[2]

2. The date of the German edition is 1867; there is also an English translation. The second book slept even longer; it was first published at Amsterdam by Professor W. Caland in 1926.

Ziegenbalg was a great man, but his repute as a writer has been somewhat cast into the shade by that of one of the most exact and percipient observers who have ever lived. The Abbé J. A. Dubois went to India as a missionary in 1792 and served for just over thirty years. Shortly before he left India he placed in the hands of the British government in Madras the revised manuscript of a remarkable book in French on *Hindu Manners, Customs, and Ceremonies*. A distinguished Indian has written of the author:

> The difficulties which a foreigner has of understanding the inner life and modes of thought of a people to which he does not belong may indeed be said to be immense. The Abbé surmounted these difficulties by devoting thirty years of his life to his subject. To effect his purpose he adopted the garb, the manners, and, as he says, even the prejudices of the people among whom his lot was cast; won their respect and confidence, and was held by them in quite as much reverence as one of their *yogis* or *gurus*.[3]

Ethnology, including the study of what are sometimes called the primitive religions, is one of the youngest of the sciences. One of its first great monuments is E. B. Tylor's classic work, *Primitive Culture* (1871). Missionaries were among the first to take advantage of the new methods and to produce a memorable series of monographs on peoples in different parts of the world. It is a tribute to the excellence of their work that many of these books are being reprinted, not by missionary but by scientific societies, fifty years after their original appearance.

Eighteen seventy-one, the year in which Tylor's great book was published, was also the year in which the young

3. Dewan Bahadur Srinavasan Raghave Iyengar C.I.E. quoted in J. A. Dubois, *Hindu Manners, Customs, and Ceremonies* (ed. of 1906), p. xxii.

bishop of Melanesia, John Coleridge Patteson, was murdered by the inhabitants of the island of Nukapu, in vengeance for the kidnapping of five of the islanders by the "black-birders." Patteson was a most unusual man. In the days when missionaries mostly wore top hats and long black coats he habitually went about in a shirt and a pair of trousers, and barefoot except when crossing a coral reef. He was one of the first to take a high view of the capacity of the Melanesians and to insist that they must be allowed to develop as Melanesians and not be turned into a travesty of the white man. He had extraordinary linguistic ability, could speak six of the Melanesian languages fluently, and could make himself understood in fourteen others. He was a friendly, tolerant, and at times amused observer of the habits and manners of his people. Many vivid touches of observation come out in his letters; but he produced no systematic work on the thought-world of the island peoples.

This task was to be taken up and accomplished by a younger colleague of Patteson, R. H. Codrington, earlier a Fellow of Wadham College, Oxford, who had been resident in the islands from 1863 till 1887. With true modesty Codrington expresses his regret that "my own time of learning has been all too short"—it was only twenty-four years—"but the writer is persuaded that one of the first duties of a missionary is to try to understand the people among whom he works, and to this end he hopes that he may have contributed something that may help." He is inclined to think that some of the darker sides of island life may have escaped him, "and the view given seems generally more favourable than might be expected; if it be so I shall not regret it." Codrington was privileged to add to the vocabulary of science a term which is now almost universally used by ethnologists, *māna,* the Melanesian word for that mysterious, uncanny power which seems to reside in certain objects or people. For good measure he added to his studies a charming collection of island tales.[4]

If we want to know about the Baganda, we must go to the Anglican Roscoe; about the Basuto to the French Protestant Casalis; about the Ila-speaking tribes of Northern Rhodesia to the Primitive Methodist E. W. Smith. The list is almost endless. But by common consent the highest prize of all goes to the Swiss Henri Alexandre Junod for his book *The Life of a South African Tribe*. Junod was born in 1863 and went to Mozambique in the service of the Swiss Mission in 1889. In 1895 a chance remark turned his attention from entomology, in which he was no mean expert, to ethnology; his great book appeared in 1912. Junod lived among the Bathonga people for thirty-two years. He lived, he listened, he analyzed, he recorded. In the words of one who has studied his work with care and affection, "the man of science and the man of imagination seem to have merged into one inspired seeker after truth, while the missionary of Calvinistic antecedents falls silent, suspending judgment until the fascinating process of learning shall have been completed."[5] The sense in which Junod viewed his own work is summed up in two brief phrases which are attributed to him: "May God preserve the life of the South African Tribe!"; "Africa would no longer be Africa if there were no more Africans."

If we are satisfied that we know something about the people, we must go on to the question of what we propose to do with, or for, them now that a measure of communication has been established. A great deal of Christian work

4. R. H. Codrington, D.D., *The Melansians: Studies in their Anthropology and Folklore* (Oxford, 1891), reprinted as one of the *Behavior Science Reprints* (New Haven, 1957).
5. Keith Irvine, in H. A. Junod, *The Life of a South African Tribe* (New York: University Books, 1962), 1:xiii.

overseas has had to do with simple peoples, or with the poor and disinherited sections of great populations, such as the so-called outcastes in India. Almost the first question that arose was, "Which comes first, civilization or the Gospel? Do we begin with men's souls, or do we first set to work to improve their social conditions, and then come on to the religious aspect of life?"

Many missionaries started out with the idea that civilization must precede evangelization. When the work was started in the Pacific islands, some of the pioneers were artisans, whose task was to teach the people arts and crafts as a means of preparing the way for those who would introduce them to the Gospel. The apostle of New Zealand, Samuel Marsden, who had revolutionized the economy of Australia by introducing merino sheep, had the same idea for the New Zealand mission which was started in 1814. Missionaries among the depressed classes in India fell into two distinct groups, a rather vocal group which maintained that social reform must precede the preaching of the Gospel and a quieter group which held the exactly contrary view.

After more than a century it is possible on purely empirical grounds to pronounce a judgment on the two methods. Experience has shown that the order of priority must always be first conversion and then social change; if the inner transformation has been brought about, the problem of social change and uplift can be tackled with far greater prospects of success. The old principle of the Gospel, "Seek ye first the kingdom of God and his righteousness, and all these things shall be added unto you," has proved itself to be not a remote and distant ideal but the most practical of advice.

This is the first and great principle. The second, which follows hard upon it, is that nothing must be done for people which they can do for themselves and that Christians must learn to support themselves without becoming dependent on the mission. It was at this point that applications of the sound principle proved much less simple and ready to hand than had been hoped.

In almost all the countries in which missionaries have worked the social system is so tightly knit that it is extraordinarily difficult for a convert to break out of it. It seems an obvious thing to teach boys to work with their hands. In fact mission industrial schools have produced a number of excellent carpenters. But where are they to find employment? In India the craftsmen are all organized in castes in which the employment is hereditary and skill is passed on from generation to generation. A carpenter of another caste, however skillful, simply cannot break into the ring. Could not the Christians, then, make an agreement to employ the Christian carpenters? But would it be really Christian to throw Hindu carpenters out of work in order to benefit Christians? Many of the boys trained in the mission schools could find employment only on the tea estates where the managers were Europeans. The growth of cities in which the caste traditions are much less rigidly maintained is helping towards a solution of this problem.

The greater part of the world's population lives by agriculture, most of it on an extremely primitive level. This seemed to be an area in which the missions ought to come to the help of the people and by improving agricultural methods to bring them to a higher standard of living. But the difficulties have proved greater than can be imagined by anyone who has not had to face them directly. In the first place peasants all over the world are extremely conservative and are not always pleased to be told that someone thinks he knows how to do their job better than they.

An agricultural school is extremely expensive to run. If we run it efficiently, we are likely to use methods and machines which simply will not be available to the pupils when they return to their villages. And we find all too often that, after a year or two in school, the boys do not want to return to their villages—they have seen something better and now want to be employed in "the mission." Yet the missionaries have not allowed themselves to be daunted by these difficulties.

At one end the missions have developed great institutions, such as the Christian Agricultural Institute at Allahabad, built up by the genius of Dr. Sam Higginbottam and later under the direction of Mr. Henry Azariah, the third son of the great Bishop Azariah of Dornakal. Here the aim was to train men on the highest possible level of agricultural skill without losing sight of the villages and their needs. These were to be the aristocrats of the agricultural enterprise, the teachers of others, and the servants of the government in its attempts to raise the agricultural level of the country.

Perhaps even more successful have been some enterprises right at the other end of the scale, such as the rural center developed by the YMCA at Martandam in Travancore under the skilled guidance of Dr. Spencer Hatch. It was Hatch's intention to do everything on the village level, to show the villagers what they could do themselves with the means and implements that they had to their hands, if they would use their minds and see how better use could be made of the materials already at their disposal—better seed selection to improve yield, planting of trees so that firewood would be available and that the invaluable cow dung could go back into the fields as manure instead of being burned as fuel in the homes, breeding of poultry from better stocks, and so on and so forth. It is a long, slow business changing the ways and the minds of villagers, but whatever is achieved is solid and of permanent worth.

The wise principle has been that nothing should be done for the people which they can do for themselves. But there are certain things which simple people cannot do for themselves and in relation to which help can rightly be given.

All peoples have some medical knowledge. The view is gaining ground that the African medicine man has acquired much empirical knowledge of the healing power of plants and roots, of which Western medicine might well take advantage. But among simple peoples life is short and hazardous, infant mortality is extremely high, and there are many situations in which they simply do not know what to do. Here, ready to hand, is a field of practical Christian service.

In the early days the missionaries had perforce to be their own doctors; they lived many miles away from the nearest medical aid. Equipped with Quain's *Dictionary of Medicine* and a large stock of familiar remedies, they brought children into the world, cared for one another, and somehow managed to survive. Livingstone in one of his letters vividly describes his wife dragging him all round the room in an effort to extract a tooth. There is a tragic story of a British missionary in Central Africa who accidentally shot himself through the arm. The only possibility of saving his life was that his wholly untrained younger colleague should amputate his arm under his direction without the help of anesthetics. Astonishingly, the operation was performed successfully, but the patient succumbed to shock and died a few days later. It is not surprising that the missionaries, having to do so much for themselves and for one another, soon found themselves engaged in giving such help as they could supply to the folks around them who fell sick.

The early attempts were highly amateurish. But by the middle of the nineteenth century the place of the trained and competent doctor in the mission was fully established. At one time the mission hospital was thought of primarily as a means of contact with the people in areas where any form of Christian work was particularly difficult. In Iran, for example, the hospital has always been at the center of the mission. The famous eye-surgeon, Sir Henry Holland, served for more than fifty years on the northwest frontier of India, where Islam makes any Christian approach extremely difficult, performing hundreds of operations every year and becoming famous throughout the length and breadth of the land. Medical work was now understood not simply as caring for those who had fallen sick but as part of the restoring power of the Gospel—preventing disease, introducing better methods of hygiene and of child care, and so helping Christian communities to lead healthy and well-developed lives to the glory of a God who cares for the bodies as well as for the souls of men.

Archbishop William Temple used to say that Christianity is the most materialistic of all the great religions of the world. By this he meant that it takes the doctrine of creation seriously, and pays great attention to man in his physical existence and in his material environment. Its most sacred ceremony is concerned with those very material things, bread and wine, and those physical acts, eating and drinking. What it believes in is not the immortality of the soul but the resurrection of the body. No apology is needed, therefore, for the amount of space we have devoted to that aspect of missionary work which deals with men's bodies and their physical environment. But man is more than a body; he has also a mind. Throughout history there has been a close connection between the Church and education.

Here the policy of the Protestant missions has been rather different from that of the Roman Catholics. The early Roman Catholic missionaries came mainly from Portugal, Spain, and Italy, where the priest was accustomed to being surrounded by an illiterate peasantry. It did not seem strange to have the same situation prevail in Africa or Asia. Education was to be largely through the eye and the ear, through the brilliant ceremonies of the Mass and the constant repetition of the catechism. There were certain partial exceptions to this general tendency in education. In the Jesuit "Reductions"—the central villages—in Paraguay scattered Indians were brought together to live under the watchful and authoritarian eye of a resident Jesuit Father. Elsewhere, where Roman Catholic educational work developed, it was largely with a view to meeting the need of the church for indigenous priests or catechists.

In Protestant work church and school have always gone hand in hand. The first Protestant mission station in India was Tranquebar, founded in 1706. A few years ago twenty-one coats of whitewash were removed from an ancient building, and there over the door was found the inscription *Dharmappallikkudam,* "free school"—it was the original school building put up by the missionaries as soon as they had any children to teach.

From small beginnings a great tree has grown. In many areas the beginnings were unbelievably small: teachers who themselves were ignorant and untrained, buildings which were little better than bush huts, where there were no buildings at all schools held under trees, children who came hungry and were liable to be withdrawn by their parents at any moment if the harvest had to be gathered or if any other urgent need had to be met. When, in East Africa, the colonial government began to take an interest in education, many of the bush schools of the missions were graded as "sub-sub-standard"! It would be hard to imagine a lower qualification. And yet the missionaries persisted. They were determined that their people should have the Word of God in their own hands and should be able to read it. Day schools were supplemented with night schools and with special instruction in the homes for those who could not go out. Dr. Frank Laubach set in motion a great campaign for the spread of literacy; while his work was highly approved by governments, it was among missionaries that he found his earliest and most practical supporters.

Then came the greatest revolution of all—the missionaries insisted that girls should learn no less than boys. This was unheard of and unimaginable; for what in the world could a woman need learning? In Hindu and Muslim society it was a rare thing for a woman to be able to read. In the villages the people protested bitterly; they needed the services of the girls at home; girls could not be allowed to waste their time on useless schooling. This was not altogether unreasonable. In a primitive society everyone works, and everyone knows what his business is. The little girl of three years old will have a job—it may be no more than sweeping up leaves, but it is a clearly understood duty and it has to be done. Some years ago, when a kindly colonial government introduced an ordinance forbidding child labor in the tin-mining district of the Bauchi highlands of Nigeria, the miners went on strike. They said, "In the village the whole family works together; if you will not let our children work with us here, we will not work either." The missionaries saw the point, but at the same time they were determined that the girls should have the opportunity of learning. Instead of the girls paying fees to come to school, the missionaries paid the parents for the loss of their children's time!

WHAT THE MISSIONARIES DID RIGHT

We have already mentioned the alliance between governments and missions and the dangers that may result when missions become financially dependent on government money. Here the other side of the coin has to be shown. Few Christians in the West are aware of the gigantic scale on which the missions have been enabled to work in the field of education. The figures for the year 1966 from the diocese of Tinnevelly, South India, show that in the Christian organization from kindergarten up to University College no less than 112,817 pupils were receiving education. About 40 percent of these are Christian, the majority are non-Christian. Most remarkable is the fact that the boys do not greatly outnumber the girls, 64,123 as against 48,694. These schools are served by an army of 3,000 teachers, almost all of whom are Christians.

The effect of this gigantic effort is seen in the standard of literacy achieved in the church. In India as a whole not more than 25 percent of the population is as yet literate. Although Christians are drawn mostly from the poorest sections of the population, the church comes third among all the communities in India in point of literacy; only the Brahmans, the traditional guardians of learning, and the small and wealthy community of the Parsis in Bombay stand higher. The diocese of Tinnevelly claims nearly 70 percent literacy among Christians over the age of five. Then too, a large proportion of Christians has gone beyond the elementary stage; a Christian middle class of professional people—teachers, doctors, lawyers, bankers, administrators—has come into being and has spread all over India in the pursuit of its professional avocations. More than thirty years ago I worked carefully through the census report of 1932 and ascertained that even then in the whole of South India there was not a community of 5,000 people in which Christians were not to be found, even though there might be no church in the place and though no mission might ever have included it in its field of work.

The wisest among the early missionaries foresaw that the foreign missionary should be only a temporary phenomenon, and that the time must come when the new churches should be able to stand on their own feet with their own bishops and presidents and moderators, their own synods and constitutions, their own ways of worship, and their own understanding of the Christian faith.

The old Lutheran mission in South India ordained a small number of Indian pastors from 1733 onwards. These were mostly catechists of long experience, who had had little formal training but were ordained on the ground of tested character and capacity. A later generation tended to think that a candidate for ordination should have the same qualifications as his missionary friends, should know Greek and Hebrew, and should be able to stand on the same intellectual level with them. With this in view William Carey brought into being in 1819 his great college at Serampore and Bishop Middleton his foundation of Bishop's College, Calcutta. This was a splendid ideal but it came a century too early. The little struggling churches simply could not produce the required number of students. Only in the twentieth century were these institutions able to fulfil the functions for which they had originally been created. For the time being an entirely different type of minister was needed.

The battle for the village ministry was fought by two now forgotten men. Gaston de Marion Brésillac (1813–59) from the south of France had dedicated himself to missionary work in India with the expressed intention, noted down in writing, of making the principal object of his work the creation of an Indian clergy. Reaching India in 1842

at the early age of thirty-two he was created (1845) Vicar
Apostolic for the area of Coimbatore, two hundred miles
southwest of Madras. He thought, optimistically, that what
was obvious to him would be obvious also to his brethren.
His purpose was to find Indians who would be able, not to
rule over large areas and to maintain considerable dignity
as the missionaries did, but to work on the same level as
the simple country priest on whom the life of the church
in France depended. Why expect of the priest in India
standards higher than those required in Europe? His colleagues would not hear of it. They assured him that no
such Indians were to be found, that the plan was premature
and could result only in grave harm to the church. After
ten years of frustration the young bishop resigned (1855),
later to find an honored grave, after no more than a few
weeks in West Africa, as the founder of the Roman Catholic
Mission to Sierra Leone.

Just at the same time, also in South India, a Welsh
missionary named John Thomas found himself dealing with
a mass movement into the church. He was a man of deep
convictions, strong character and tireless diligence. I am
fortunate in possessing what must be an almost unique
copy of letters written in India a hundred years ago—
Letters of Arnold Christian Pears published privately in
Madras in 1931. Colonel Pears, after retirement from the
army, became an inspector of schools and later postmaster
general of Madras. As inspector he had to visit the various
mission stations and has left behind vivid accounts of what
he found. He arrived at Megnanapuram, where Thomas
lived, on Good Friday 1860 and tells us much of what he
found there. Of the church he says, "Our engineers have
never produced anything to be compared with it in any
respect. . . . I find the boarding schools here the best that I
have ever seen." But he learned that Thomas sometimes

65

had problems to deal with and was prepared to deal with them in a somewhat individual and forceful way:

> I asked whether he had not found some difficulty in getting his schoolboys to work so cheerfully and diligently as they did in his garden every morning. He told me that they did not like it at first, and that one boy had once refused to work. He went on in his usual measured and decided tone, "I sent for him and said 'What is this, boy? Do you say you will not work?' 'No, Sir, why should I work? I came to school to learn and not to work in the garden.' " He expected (Thomas went on) a mild expostulation, some kind of Christian counsel on the duty of obedience, but he *received* a box on the ear which felled him to the ground. They have all worked very happily ever since.[6]

It was this slightly militant Christian who set to work to fight the great battle for a true village ministry for village people. He maintained the thesis that the church ought to take the best of the village catechists, give them a thorough training in their own language, and then ordain them to the full work of the ministry in the villages. Tamil is a highly developed, copious, and beautiful language; there is no theological idea that cannot be expressed in it; why should it be thought that English is the only language in which sound Protestant theology can be conveyed? The idea was new, and like all new ideas met with vigorous opposition—such men would never command the respect of the villagers, the whole idea of the sacred ministry would be lowered, and so on and so forth. But Thomas was not to be so easily overcome. He could not fell his opponents to the ground with a single blow, but he could and did wear them out by patience and argument. At last it was agreed,

6. C. D. Pears, *Letters of Arnold Christian Pears* (Madras, 1931), p. 146.

and the first class of six men was formed in 1846 and met in the tower room of the church which later was to be the cathedral of the diocese. The village ministry was in being.

Once these men had been ordained, they were so extra-ordinarily successful that no question of their suitability to their high office was ever raised again. Of one of them, John Thomas, wrote:

> I never listened with such unfeigned pleasure to any other preacher. He was a profound divine, handling the most difficult questions with astonishing ease and clearness. . . . The impression upon my mind was, this man is at perfect ease when descanting upon the mysteries of religion, and has penetrated further within the veil than anyone I ever met before. . . . His imagination was fertile, his resources in illustration copious, appropriate and euphonious in the highest degree.[7]

All this is said of a man who could not speak a word of English and had been educated only in his own native Tamil. Others heard of what had happened in South India. The principle that knowledge of a Western language is not to be regarded as a requirement for ordination came to be accepted almost everywhere in the world.

To have brought into being this village ministry was a splendid achievement. But clearly things could not rest there. When a certain level of education had become general, Western languages came to be used for the instruction of those who could profit by them. The next step, taken in the twentieth century, was the setting up or reviving of theological seminaries in which men could study for the ministry on the same level as their missionary colleagues.

7. Eugene Stock, *History of the Church Missionary Society* (1899), 2:184.

Africa has fallen rather behind in the race. But almost every country in Asia today, and several in Latin America, have at least one seminary on this level. Nor have the Roman Catholics fallen behind. And the number of students who have received the highest training available in their own countries and have then come on to complete their studies in the seminaries of the West is steadily increasing. When such leaders are available, the question at once arises whether the missionary has not fulfilled his own ideal and worked himself out of a job.

"The church is there; the missionary can now quietly disappear." Is this a logical sequence of thought? This was the opinion of Henry Venn and his contemporaries. As soon as the church is established, the foreign missionary should sever his connection and look for other fields to plough. Experience, however, has shown that, reasonable as this argument has seemed to be, the obvious logical conclusion is not that which should be drawn. From some situations the missionary ought certainly to disappear; in others his task is not so much to disappear as to change his role. When new liberty is being given to a church, that is the time not to diminish but to increase the number of foreign workers.

The member or minister of a younger church who is appointed to supreme leadership in a church or in a great institution is faced by a situation of serious difficulty. He has to take up heavy responsibilities, for which it may well be that he has had no really adequate training. He has now to make the decisions which in the past have always been made for him, and it will be impossible to conceal the fact that it is he who has decided and no one else. It is unlikely that his appointment to the post he holds has been unanimously agreed upon; there will be discontented people who will be only too happy to see him stumble. A lonely position, and one in which a man is only too thankful to have some friends on whose discretion he can absolutely rely. In case after case it has been the foreigner who, just because he stands a little remote from local feelings and problems, is able to supply the need.

A great step forward was taken in the history of the Anglican Church in India when in 1912 Vedanayakam Samuel Azariah was appointed to be its first Indian bishop. An Anglican bishop must necessarily bear a heavy weight of responsibility. The clergy look up to him as their head, and the laity expect him to give the lead in a great many matters affecting the welfare of the Church in every direction. Azariah was only thirty-eight years old when he was consecrated Bishop of Dornakal. He knew that a large number of missionaries had been against the appointment, regarding it as premature. He knew also that many Indian Christian leaders looked down on him because he was not from the higher castes. It needed great courage to take up such a load.

But Azariah was a man of great courage. One mark of this courage was that he was not afraid of Western missionaries and was able to use them in the service of the Church. For twenty years of his episcopate he was served by three European archdeacons, all men of exceptional ability but of remarkably different gifts, who were prepared to take from the bishop's hands almost all the troublesome details of finance and administration, to stand completely in the background, and to let the bishop concentrate on the work of teaching and preaching for which he was so admirably endowed. In the years that followed Azariah was a renowned and accepted speaker at almost every ecumenical conference—Lausanne 1927, Edinburgh 1937, Tambaram 1938. Few of those who heard him thought to ask how it was that the bishop was able to spend so much time away from his diocese. Of those who knew his name not one in a hundred could have mentioned the name of a single one of his archdeacons. Yet it is certain that without their utterly devoted and self-effacing service his great work could not have been accomplished.

To stay may be harder than to go. It is easy to say, "He must increase and I must decrease"; it is not always so easy to put this excellent principle into practice. Yet self-effacement may be at this point the greatest of Christian virtues. "There was a little city, and few men within it; and there came a great king against it, and besieged it, and built great bulwarks against it: now there was found in it a poor wise man, and he by his wisdom delivered the city; yet no man remembered that same poor man." [8]

8. Ecclesiastes 9:14–15.

4

Where Do We Go from Here?

In 1800 Christianity was almost exclusively the white man's religion. The Atlantic Ocean had become the inland sea of the Christian peoples; such other Christians as there were lived in odd corners here and there, far from the main streams of the Christian world. In a single century the entire situation has been changed. As a result of the success of the world mission of the nineteenth century, by 1910, the year of the first World Missionary Conference held in Edinburgh, Christianity had become for the first time in its history a worldwide religion.

The conference met on a flood tide of confidence and joyful expectation. The success of the mission had far surpassed anything that had been foreseen. For thirty years Dr. John R. Mott, the chairman, had been proclaiming throughout the world the slogan "The Evangelization of the World in this Generation"; the time had come to take stock of what had actually been achieved. Mott was a great idealist, but he was not starry-eyed, as has sometimes been supposed. He was the most practical of men; he never confused evangelization with conversion. Nowhere in his many writings is there any suggestion that the whole world could be *converted* in a single generation—human freedom, if nothing else would see to that. What Mott was concerned about was the preaching of the Gospel to every nation;

71

he never wavered in his conviction that, if the Christian churches would do their duty, the whole world could become in a generation the parish of the Christian mission. Looking back over the developments of a hundred years, he could adduce powerful arguments in favor of his view.

1) The whole world had become accessible to an extent to which there had been no parallel in history. To verify this, the reader need do no more than go to the nearest large public library and ask to see an atlas published a century ago; he will find vast areas in Africa marked "unexplored." Less than a century has passed since Stanley's great journey of 999 days in which he ascertained in detail the course of the Congo River. The centenary of the arrival of the first missionaries in Uganda (1876) has not yet been observed.

The agelong methods of slow travel were being replaced by the steamboat and the railway train. In the year before the conference, Blériot had flown the English Channel, but no one then dreamed of the influence that air travel would have on Christian history. What had been already achieved was sensational enough. Before the railway reached Tinnevelly in South India in 1867, it was reckoned that the journey by bullock cart from Madras would take a month; now the missionary could travel by train and arrive in twenty-four hours.

2) The problems of tropical disease and of the health of white men in the tropics had almost been solved. Even in the second half of the nineteenth century deaths and breakdowns in the missionary ranks were very frequent. To look through the list of missionaries of any missionary society is to see how few of them lived out a full term of service. Such great discoveries as the determination of the cause of malaria by Sir Ronald Ross in the 1890s were making it possible for the white man to face almost any

climate in the world with a fair prospect of survival, provided that reasonable caution was observed. What used to be called "the white man's grave," the West Coast of Africa, is today setting itself to develop a tourist trade on a large scale; this had not been thought of in 1910, but already the situation was entirely different from what it had been in 1810.

3) When missionaries have to start by learning a language that has never been reduced to writing, many years must pass before they can converse fluently with the people they have come to win, and with some assurance that the message they desire to communicate will really be understood. By 1900 all the main languages of the world had been studied, and grammars and dictionaries were available for those who would learn them.

4) Not merely so, the New Testament had been translated into so many languages that more than three-quarters of the people in the world, if literate, had access to the whole New Testament and many more to at least a Gospel. In 1910 some part of the Bible was already available in more than six hundred languages.

5) When the modern missionary enterprise began, it was viewed with considerable suspicion by the churches; the work was left for the most part in the hands of small groups of "friends of missions." By 1910 the churches, with the American churches in the van, had begun to see that the mission is so much an essential part of the life of the church that a church with no share in the missionary enterprise can only doubtfully claim to be a church.

6) In consequence large sums of money had begun to flow into the coffers of the missionary societies. The societies and the missionaries they supported had never been wealthy. The great David Livingstone was expected by the London Missionary Society to support himself and his

family on $500 a year; money was worth a great deal more then than it is today, but even that thrifty Scot maintained that it just could not be done. Most of the German missionaries in India had to find some form of additional work in order to keep alive; not much was left over for developing the work of the mission. Critics who have asked why the missionaries did not do this or that have often failed to take the financial factor into account—to ask how much would have been required and from what sources it could conceivably have come. But, with the new sense of responsibility dawning in the churches, a great deal was becoming possible that could not earlier have been thought of.

7) With this wider interest went a large increase in the number of missionaries and a notable improvement in their quality. Few of the early missionaries were university graduates. In spite of this some of them developed into notable scholars. Edward Sell, who lived for sixty years in Madras and before the end of his life had earned a string of honorary doctorates as an expert in Islam, in his youth had never set foot in a university. But these were the exceptions. Most missionaries of the nineteenth century were humble folk by origin, and few of them attained to notable distinction. By the turn of the century the situation had largely changed. Many of the ablest students from the universities of the West were finding their way into missionary service.

8) Most important of all, the new missionary on arrival in his field of service, would not find himself alone in a strange land; there would be colleagues from a newly planted church to welcome him. In almost every country in the world the Church had begun to take root. No race had ever been found which, however primitive, was incapable of understanding the gospel; no religion in the world had failed to yield some converts to the Church. There was

still plenty of pioneer work to be done; but in most parts of the world there were at least some foundations on which the missionary could build.

This was an impressive list of achievements, especially when account is taken of the small number of missionaries engaged in the work and of the limited resources at their disposal. It is not surprising that those who attended the conference of 1910 felt their spirits bowed in awe as they contemplated the greatness of what God had wrought, and that they looked forward with sober optimism to uninterrupted and more rapid progress until the end of the twentieth century. We must turn now to the disasters which they could not have forseen.

Though there were in 1910 these many grounds for hope, it was not by any means a time for unqualified optimism. Heavy clouds were gathering around the ship of faith.

The first warning sign had been given in 1905 when Japan totally defeated Russia. Some were hardly disturbed by this, reckoning Russia to be a backward nation which hardly deserved to be reckoned as part of either Christendom or Europe. Those more sensitive to currents of feeling in Asia and Africa realized that this event marked already the beginning of the end of colonialism.

It was in Russia once again that the second deadly blow was dealt to Christendom as the nineteenth century had known it. In the early days of the war of 1914 to 1918 the czar Nicholas II had been astonished at the outburst of spontaneous loyalty and affection for himself as the representative of Holy Russia, which had been evident in many cities and in the countryside. By 1917 all was changed. The old empire had come to an end, to be succeeded by the horrors of the civil war and then by the bleak and cheerless dialectic of Marxism. Russia, which had believed itself to be charged with the mission of bringing back to a paganized West the light of the Gospel, now seemed to be setting itself to the task of extinguishing that light wherever it was to be found. The Russian Church had ceased before 1910 to be a missionary church, but it had still been a force in Christendom; after the Revolution of 1917 the kingdom of Christ in the world appeared to be mutilated by the almost total loss of these great Eastern provinces.

Worse was to follow in the next half century as country after country in Eastern and Central Europe fell under Communist domination. In some ways the worst blow of all came with the Communist coup in China. For more than a century China had been the principal interest of the United States overseas. The churches had poured out their resources with exemplary generosity, in missionary effort, in the building up of the YMCA and the YWCA in all the principal cities of China, in the bringing of innumerable Chinese students to America for higher training in every form of academic and practical discipline. It was hard to see this immense investment go, as it seemed irreversibly, down the drain. Worse even than the expulsion of all missionaries was the venom of bitter accusation and recrimination with which even well-balanced Chinese Christians seemed to pursue their former friends.

All this should not be taken more tragically than it deserves. Communists have expected that every form of religion would disappear within a few years in face of the advancing tide of science. They are beginning to discover that the Christian faith is an anvil which has worn out many hammers. The churches have no doubt been gravely weakened, but they have not been annihilated. The decision of the Orthodox Churches in Russia and other Communist-controlled countries to become member churches of the

World Council of Churches (1961) indicates that these groups recognize a Christian loyalty which is strong enough to overcome the division caused by differing political allegiances. Whenever a message comes from Christians in China (and over the last ten years this has happened only rarely) it is always to the same effect, "We belong together; we pray for you; pray for us."

China is not the only country in which today the Christian forces live and work under difficulties. A number of the newly independent nations, while recording the principle of religious freedom in their constitution, are yet placing many difficulties in the way of Christian missionary work and of the residence of missionaries within their territories. Among these is India, a secular democratic republic which prides itself on being completely tolerant in matters of religion, yet is making it daily more difficult for missionaries to enter the country. Not long ago a young man who had qualified both in agriculture and in theology was assigned to an agricultural mission in India. It might be thought that this was exactly the kind of help that India needed today; but at the last moment permission to reside in India was refused, and this promising candidate had to transfer his offer of service to Zambia.

Burma has gone rather further than India. No foreigner can reside in the country for any purpose of religious propaganda. The Burmese churches, which fortunately had been well-prepared by the missionaries for independence, have had to learn to stand entirely on their own feet. The Republic of Guinea in West Africa has gone even further. All foreign missionaries, most of whom were Roman Catholics, were required to leave the country. When the Roman Catholic authorities moved in experienced African Christians from other countries, the government pointed out that the black man no less than the white could be a foreigner, and these emergency helpers also had to be withdrawn.

Nationalism in many countries has found an expression in the revival of the ancient religions. The aim of many Buddhists in Ceylon is to make of that island a unitary state, with one people, one state, one language, one culture, and one religion, regardless of the fact that more than a million people on the island speak Tamil and not Sinhalese, and that there are considerable Christian, Hindu, and Muslim minorities.

All these new factors should be sufficient to convince the Christian that there is no place in the modern world for an unthinking optimism. Some Christians have gone much further than this and for some reason are spreading abroad in the Christian world a spirit of pessimism and defeatism.

One form of this pessimism is observable in the affirmation that, though the number of Christians in the world is increasing, as a result of the population explosion in the non-Christian countries the Christian percentage of the world's population has already begun to decrease and will continue to grow less until the end of the century. One Christian writer of considerable eminence has stated confidently that, whereas the Christian percentage was about 33 in 1940, it has now fallen below 30 and will not be more than 16 in the year 2000. A more radical estimate is that by that date Christians will be no more than one in ten among the peoples of the world.

Although asserted with such confidence these estimates appear to have been put forward on the basis only of guesswork and not of careful study of such figures as are available. In projections of figures of population, allowance must always be made for wide margins of error, since there are so many factors of uncertainty. But recently for the first time an attempt has been made to arrive at a scientific estimate, based on population figures supplied by the United Nations and on the best available statistics from Christian sources. These present a very different picture. It appears that in the past the Christian percentage has been overestimated, since the population of China, almost entirely non-Christian, is now held to be larger than was earlier supposed. When the necessary corrections have been made, the conclusion is reached that the percentage has been slowly increasing since the beginning of the century, is slowly increasing, and will continue to increase; so that, if present trends continue, it will in the year 2000 stand higher than ever before in the history of the world. What is a little startling is that at that date less than half the Christians will belong to the white races.

Of course nothing much is gained by knowing how many nominal Christians there are in the world; the churches live only in the lives of their devoted and committed members. But the same, of course, is true also of Hinduism and of Islam. For the purpose of comparative statistics it is necessary to include all those who regard themselves as adherents of one creed rather than another. If they do nothing more, these carefully calculated figures at least show us that there is no ground for the alarming picture of decline with which the Christian pessimists have been inclined to terrify us.

Another bogey is the alleged success of Islam in Africa. The impression has been given that Islamic missions in Africa have been far more successful than Christian. Wide currency has been given to the affirmation that every year five times as many Africans become Muslims as become Christians. This affirmation will not stand up for a moment when confronted by the facts. It is undoubtedly the case that in some areas, principally in the former French colonies where Islam is already strongly entrenched, that faith is extending its sway to tribes which had not previously been touched. But it would be a grave mistake to generalize from these limited areas to the continent as a whole. The actual fact is that in such territories as Zambia, Rhodesia, and the Congo, Islam is hardly known. On the East Coast which has been visited by Arab traders for more than a thousand years, Islam is powerful in the coastal areas, especially in Tanzania, but this influence dwindles the further we go inland from the coast. In an area such as Eastern Nigeria, where busy Muslim missionaries have been building mosques all over the place, the Christianization of the population has gone so far that the mosques remain for the most part empty.

There is reason to think that Islam has already passed the highest point of its appeal to Africa. It was strongly favored by the colonial powers—by the Germans in Tanzania, by the French everywhere, by the British in Northern Nigeria. This gave it prestige. The African who became a Muslim felt himself to be rising in the social scale, and at the cost of a far smaller disruption of his preexisting life than was demanded by Christianity. He was entering into a great international brotherhood, yet at the same time retaining much of his tribal existence intact. But does Islam offer what Africa wants today? The language provides an acid test. Today a great many Africans are eager to learn German, since Germany has a reputation as the great land of technical skills. A smaller but still considerable number are learning Russian. But who wants to learn Arabic? It is a great and splendid language and, within limits, international; but it does not hold the key to those new worlds to the conquest of which the African is setting himself. For good or ill the destiny of Africa is linked with the West. Whether that destiny will be Christian or merely materialistic depends to a considerable extent on the way in which the Christian churches play their cards in the coming thirty years.

So much for the negative side. We find no reason to despair. But have we any positive grounds for hope? Is there any reason to suppose that the Christian mission in the closing years of the twentieth century is something other than a futile waste of time? A glance at four areas, of which three are south of the equator, may serve to outline an answer to this question.

Taiwan, that beautiful island which we used to call Formosa, has had a restless history. For fifty years it was under the Japanese who, as everywhere else, proved themselves efficient colonists, but harsh and unsympathetic in their attitude to those whom they ruled. When the Japanese were driven out, rule over Taiwan returned to the Chinese; but hardly had this been accomplished when the Communist coup on the mainland drove Chiang Kai-shek and more than a million of his followers to cross the sea and start a new life in Taiwan. The results were, from the Christian point of view, disturbing in the extreme. The mainland Chinese brought in with them almost every known variety of the Christian faith, so much so that within a few years two separate Lutheran seminaries grew up in an island which prior to 1949 had hardly heard that Lutherans existed. The two strongest missions had both been Presbyterian, by now happily brought together in one single church, with a much smaller Roman Catholic mission at work in the main centers.

In 1955 the Presbyterian Church of Taiwan considered the question of what it should do to celebrate its centenary, which would fall in 1965. With great daring, but without the arrogance of purely human presumption, it decided that it would double its worshipping congregations and its membership in ten years. By careful training of the laity in the art of Christian witness, by a number of well-organized campaigns, by intensive use of Christian literature, and in the main by the quiet testimony of individual Christians to non-Christian friends, the goal was reached within the appointed time, and with something to spare. It is important not to exaggerate. The number of Protestant Christians in Taiwan today is about half a million out of a total of twelve and a half million, or 4 percent. Nevertheless the achievement of the Presbyterian Church is considerable and shows what can still be accomplished by good organization and steady devotion, without the waving of any large number of flags.

Indonesia is the fifth country in the world in point of population—after China, India, Russia, and the United States. Christian missions had had notable successes in the nineteenth century, when Indonesia was controlled by the Dutch. It might have been expected that the situation would become markedly less favorable with Indonesian independence and the establishment of a republic with at least a partial recognition of Islam as the national religion. The expected has not happened. In no less than six areas of this island world, three thousand miles from northwest to southeast, considerable movements into the Church of Christ are taking place. In West Irian, that remote and mountainous region at the western end of New Guinea, which was much in the news in 1969 because of the Indonesian pledge that in that year its population would be allowed freely to pronounce on its own future, half the population is said to be already Christian. The most remarkable of all these movements is that in East Java, where many Muslims are enquiring about the Christian faith. Reports have been received of a service during which, in a single afternoon, two hundred families were admitted by baptism to the Church. It is well-known that in Indonesia Islamic faith is somewhat superficial, being deeply penetrated by the old animism of pre-Islamic days. But it seems that a movement on this scale from Islam to Christianity has hardly been known before in the entire history of the Church.

It is difficult to get accurate information about these movements in Indonesia. The authorities of the Indonesian churches are anxious not to draw too much attention to their affairs, for two reasons. There is always the danger of attracting Christian forces which pay little attention to the principle of "comity"—non-interference by one mission in an area in which another is already at work—and come in hoping to reap a quick harvest where others have sown. And the Muslim world is not unnaturally sensitive to any alleged Christian success in any land where Islam is dominant. The missionary in an Islamic country soon learns that it is prudent to write only of his work of sowing and to let his "successes" be recorded only in the ledgers of the angels.

We turn now to a very different area, Central Tanzania in East Africa. Here, too, Christian missions have been favored with considerable success. The largest church is the Roman Catholic, next to it the Lutheran. But the most remarkable growth in recent years has been recorded in the Anglican diocese of Central Tanzania. This part of the world came very much into public notice twenty years ago through the abortive plan of the British Colonial Development Corporation to grow groundnuts in an area centered on the town of Kongwa. Those who inspected the area on behalf of the corporation were delighted to find large tracts of uncultivated but apparently fertile land. It did not occur to them that the local inhabitants, the Wagogo, are no fools, and that, if land were suitable for the growing of crops, they would long ago have found out all about it. The corporation learned its lesson too late; after the expenditure of enormous sums of money the entire project had to be abandoned.

Shortly after this fiasco a new bishop, an Australian, was appointed to the diocese, of which the see city is Dodoma. A missionary of long experience in Africa, he took hold of the situation with driving dynamism, and things began to happen. Asked in 1964 what he reckoned to be the average increase in the number of Christians in his area, he answered, "9 percent per annum." The expert mathematician will calculate at once that this means that a church will double itself in seven and a half years. Four years later the bishop's figure was shown to be almost exactly accurate. In the sixteen years of his episcopate the church in the area was found to have quadrupled itself—from twenty thousand to eighty thousand. If cross-examined as to the causes of this remarkable development, the bishop would probably lay stress on four factors: (1) a powerful and convincing message leading up to personal surrender to Jesus Christ; (2) no spoon-feeding—nothing to be done for African Christians except those things that they cannot possibly do for themselves; if they want a church, let them build it themselves by cooperative effort, in the simple style that is suitable to their surroundings; (3) the missionary was to keep strictly in the background; responsibility for its own life is to be carried by the African church itself; (4) at the earliest possible date African Christians are to be taught to take up the task of bearing witness to others and so to keep the movement moving. What the bishop would not mention would be admirable and disciplined organization at the center, scrupulously careful use of funds, and the encouraging presence of a leader the heart and soul of whose own ministry is the insatiable desire that men and women should be won for Christ. It is good to be able to add, as an

84

example of international cooperation, that as a result of generous funds made available from Germany, it has been possible to revolutionize the educational work of the diocese, and so to help forward the training of those who in the days to come should be the leaders of the African church.

The fourth area of startling progress is Latin America, the greater part of which also lies south of the equator. Of this vast southern continent it is difficult to speak except in pairs of antitheses. Nowhere in the world is the contrast between wealth and poverty more bitter and grinding; yet on the whole this is a continent of hope—Latin Americans tend to compare themselves, to their own advantage, with the worn-out and degenerate peoples of the Northern Hemisphere. The term "American" suggests that North and South America belong intimately together; but in fact New York is nearer to London, Berlin, and Moscow than it is to Buenos Aires or Santiago de Chile, and most Latin Americans regard themselves as more closely akin to Europe than to the land of the *gringos* to the north. The Roman Catholic Church has traditionally been all too closely associated with the establishment and the forces of reaction; yet today some of the most passionate pleas for social reform come from bishops of that church in northern Brazil.

This is only a part of the tremendous effort being made by the Roman Catholic Church to meet the needs of an area in which the population explosion is at its maximum, in which almost everyone is nominally a Roman Catholic, but where in many areas there is hardly so much as one priest to ten thousand members of that church. It is not surprising that Protestant churches have regarded this as a field in which they may legitimately work; attempts to meet the needs of those who have been left in such total spiritual destitution can hardly be regarded as "proselytization" in any bad sense of that word. Protestant church membership has doubled and redoubled itself again and again in the course of this century.

Two major changes may be noted in Christian attitudes in Latin America. Much Protestant success has been in the underworld of misery, and here, to their eternal credit, the Pentecostalists have shown a special aptitude for making the Gospel come alive to those on the very margin of human existence. The concern of these groups is with conversion; people must be brought to a saving knowledge of Jesus Christ, and that is all. With the social and economic problems of the times they have not greatly concerned themselves. Yet, almost unawares, they have been instrumental in bringing about a great social revolution. As men and women are converted they begin to drink less and to work more. Children begin to go to school, then to high school, then to college. Within a generation or two the missions have produced a Protestant elite, thrifty, diligent, upright, and not always very much interested in looking back to the pit whence it emerged.

On both sides the churches have been in danger of indifference to the pressing needs of the time—the Roman Catholic Church because it has been all along the church of the possessing classes and the defender of the *status quo,* the Protestants because a false spirituality has led some to think that politics is a dirty game in which Christians cannot participate, and that economic problems should not too deeply interest those who are living in daily expectation of the Second Coming of Christ. Today all this is changing. Roman Catholics and Protestants alike are realizing that social justice is an integral part of the Gospel, and that, though the life of the Spirit can miraculously flourish even under the most unfavorable conditions, it is not seemly that in an age of affluence millions of human beings should be deprived of the minimum which is necessary for the normal development of the body and the mind. There was at one time a danger that progressive thinking in Latin America might be identified with the Marxist cause; today it seems that the most advanced social thinking is to be found among Christians, and that Christians may be the leaders in the much-needed campaigns for the overthrow of antiquated idols, the ending of abuses, and the introduction of freedom for peoples to whom it has been guaranteed in name but denied in fact.

It is always difficult to form a general impression of the situation in the world at any given time. The United States has reached a level of affluence unknown before in human history, yet the government finds it necessary to launch a poverty program on a large scale. Agricultural production in the West has reached a point at which we simply do not know what to do with all the food that is being produced, yet we are told that half the world goes to bed hungry every evening. There has been no major war for a quarter of a century, yet each morning as we wake we wonder what new local explosion may threaten the peace of the entire world. On what side of the picture do we look? Should we allow ourselves to sink down in utter gloom, or may we allow ourselves to entertain at least moderate hopes of a better time coming?

The same contrast confronts us when we look at the Christian world. Do we live in the twilight of the gods? Or are we seeing the gradual spreading of the light which "shineth more and more unto the perfect day"? There is always a tendency to romanticize the past and to think that things are more difficult for us than they have been for any previous generation. Readers of historical literature know that in every generation men, and Christians no less than others, have felt exactly the same.

It is not surprising that the supporters of missions in the early days of the modern missionary movement felt themselves at times daunted by difficulties and disasters to which there seemed to be no end. For fifty years Christian workers sat on the borders of China wondering whether access to that closed land would ever be granted to them. In the first twenty years of the mission to Sierra Leone the Church Missionary Society lost by death fifty-one missionaries. In India the attitude of the East India Company was so hostile that an Indian Christian could not hope for employment even in the meanest ranks of the servants of the government. In South America Captain Allen Gardiner and his companions, the pioneers of the South American Missionary Society, froze and starved to death on the hostile shores of Patagonia. All in all it was not a cheerful prospect.

While we may be inclined to romanticize the past, as Christians we are hardly likely to romanticize our present. We are faced with a rapid decline in participation in the life of the church in all the countries of Western Europe. The American churches have lost confidence and seem to exercise less influence than they did at the beginning of the century. On every American campus the student is assailed by a myriad of voices, assuring him that the Christian faith belongs to an outworn age and that the churches have fatally betrayed their trust. In the newly independent nations, nationalism, sometimes allied with the resurgence of an ancient religion, seems to bar the way to any serious consideration of the Christian Gospel. The threat of total destruction in a nuclear war tends to dismay the ardent mind and to paralyze the active arm. What can be done in such a situation?

WHERE DO WE GO FROM HERE?

Some Christians would answer that these are days in which the Church must be prepared to return to the catacombs and wait for better times. There is little that can be done, except perhaps an almost despairing maintenance of the faith and a refurbishing of weapons in the vague hope that some day the call to battle may be heard again. This is hardly an inspiring gospel for presentation to the young.

At this point it may be profitable to ask what was meant by the famous Christian scholar, Bishop J. B. Lightfoot, when he said nearly a century ago that the study of history was a cordial for drooping spirits. Lightfoot was far too great a scholar ever to have yielded to such a naïve evolutionary optimism as imagines that every day and in every way everything is getting better and better. He was far from seeing the whole panorama of history as a success story in which steadily and irreversibly darkness is overcome by light. He seems to have had in his mind two things which cannot be denied. First, it is astonishing how much can be achieved by Christians in the face of the greatest imaginable difficulties, provided they bring to the task courage, imagination, patience, and the spirit of cooperation between all the available forces. Second, history shows us again and again that, when everything seemed at its darkest, God has in the most unexpected way caused new light to shine in the darkness. With the advantage of hindsight, we can see a long process of preparation for the Reformation through the Middle Ages; yet the most optimistic prophet of reform in those times could hardly have foreseen the emergence of Martin Luther on the horizon of world history.

Christians of the twentieth century would be cowards and renegades if they allowed themselves to be so cowed by existing difficulties as to adopt the view that there is nothing to be done except to concentrate all their resources on the mere effort to survive. It may well be that we are just on the edge of one of those great epochs in which in unexpected ways God releases forces for the renewal of his Church and sends it out on new and untried ways. Whether this be so or not, in the meantime there is a great deal to be done. Our final chapter must give some pointers as to the areas in which effective and practical Christian service can be rendered in a world which day by day is inescapably being unified and of which increasingly Christians ought to feel themselves a part.

5

The Missionary

of the

Future

The reader who has followed our argument up to this point and then looks at the title of this chapter may well be inclined to ask, "Will there be any?" The missionary enterprise of the West in Africa and the East was a phenomenon belonging to a particular period of human history. Now that that period has come to an end is there any longer any occasion for that particular manifestation of Christian dynamism? Had not the Western Christian very much better stay at home?

It may be taken as certain that the missionary enterprise of the churches cannot be carried on in the future as it was carried on in the past. It will have to be radically modified in the light of extensive changes that have taken place both in the political balance of the world and in the condition of the Christian churches.

Scholars have pointed out, almost to weariness, that the rise of modern Christian missions coincided with what we have been taught to call the Vasco de Gama era in the history of the world.[1] For three centuries the Roman Catholic powers, Spain and Portugal, and rather later

1. Vasco de Gama rounded the Cape of Good Hope and anchored off Calicut in South India in 1498, thus inaugurating a new order in the relation between Europe and the East.

France, almost monopolized the missionary scene. The Protestant nations took up the cause with vigor only in the nineteenth century—but that was the period of the most rapid colonial expansion. The French in Africa and the Dutch in Indonesia were expanding their imperial domains until 1907, two years after the defeat of Russia by Japan which we noted as marking the beginning of the end of Western imperial aggression. The United States came late upon the scene, at the end of the nineteenth century in the period of "manifest destiny." Where the colonial powers were at work, Christian missions were also to be found.

A common opinion has been formed that there was at all times so close an alliance between colonial regimes and the missionary forces that the Christian enterprise can be regarded as only one more manifestation of Western aggressiveness, that without the support of the colonial powers the missions would have had no chance of success, and that with the decline of colonialism the missions also are bound to diminish and to wither away. An examination of the facts shows that the relationship was far more complicated than this, and that missionaries were as prepared to oppose their own governments, when occasion demanded, as to cooperate with them.

The first opportunity for missionaries to reside in mainland China came after the victory of Britain in the Opium War of 1840–42. Almost every writer on the subject has drawn attention to the grave disadvantages under which the missions labored through their association with Chinese defeat and humiliation. Few have recorded the torrent of Christian protest in England against what was felt to be an unjust and unnecessary war or the ceaseless activities of Christians in Britain and elsewhere on behalf of the abolition of opium-growing in India, and of the Indian traffic with China in the noxious drug. The British declaration (1923) that Kenya was African territory, and that in the case of any clash of interests those of the African population must be paramount, was obtained almost entirely as a result of missionary and Christian pressure. In the same year, 1923, Rhodesia obtained "self-government" by the white settler class; the failure of the Christian forces in one case underlines the significance of their success in the other.

Justice demands that this should be made plain. Yet the colonial powers were shrewd enough to see that in many cases they could use the missionary for the furtherance of their own purposes. In the General Act of the Berlin Conference of 1884, that charter of liberty for Africa in which the doom of the slave trade was finally sealed, the great powers of the West committed themselves to responsibility for helping and supporting Christian missions in the areas yet to be opened up, not indeed as religious agencies but as instruments for the diffusion of knowledge and civilization, a distinction which was not always clear to the inhabitants of the areas affected. In treaty after treaty between stronger and weaker powers, the obligation to permit the entry of missionaries and to maintain their rights was included in the terms. The missionary came in with the prestige of Western political and economic power. However far he was prepared to go in identifying himself with the people among whom he lived, he was still credited, and not without reason, with ready access to the representatives of the ruling power and in many cases with influence far greater than he was in reality able to exercise.

Now all that has gone. Colonialism has practically disappeared. The number of independent nations represented at the United Nations in New York increases almost every year. The missionary enters these countries, like any other foreigner resident abroad, with no special advantage and no special protection. Some nations refuse to admit him at all or lay down conditions which make his residence difficult. He is at all times dependent on the good will of the local government. If his conduct in any particular does not please the authorities, he is liable at any moment to be deported as an undesirable alien. The freedom to go wherever he liked and, within reason, to do whatever he liked, which in the nineteenth century was guaranteed to the foreign missionary by the colonial powers, is now a thing of the past.

This is one great change in the situation. The second, equally great, is even more significant from the point of view of the Christian enterprise. The missionary of today does not go out into a vacuum. Supporters of Christian missions in the West are often unaware of the success that has been granted to these missions. In almost every country in the world thriving churches have come into being. Just as former colonies have grown into independent nations, churches which used to be extensions and dependencies of churches in the West have grown into independent, self-governing churches, managing their own affairs and demanding partnership on a basis of perfect spiritual equality with the older churches in the West. At Vatican Council II, older bishops in the West were astonished by the number of indigenous bishops from Africa and the East and still more by the vigor and independence of spirit that they manifested; they were by no means content either to be silent, or simply to echo the opinions of the representatives of the European and American churches. A great many of the Protestant churches now have membership in the World Council of Churches and regard themselves as the representatives not simply of the handful of Christians in their countries but of great and venerable civilizations. Their interest is in fellowship in a world-wide church, and not in a special relationship to a local missionary society.

There are in the West some missionary societies and churches which regard themselves as still having the right to go where they will and to do what they like, without consultation with anyone, in so far as the political situation permits. Some bodies, such as the Seventh-Day Adventists, conscientiously believe that the Gospel has nowhere really been preached unless it has been preached in the particular form to which they have given their adherence; they cannot regard themselves as bound by any agreements of "comity," noncompetition, under which many societies have limited the sphere of their activities. Other groups, largely of the "faith mission" type, tend to settle where there are already large churches in existence and to profit from discontent within Christian groups rather than to grow through direct evangelization among non-Christians. The main line churches, on the contrary, are scrupulous in recognizing the rights of the younger churches themselves, which they have been privileged to call into being: It is for them now to call the tune. It is for them to say where and whether new work should be opened up. The initiative cannot now be taken by the authorities of some distant church or mission in a Western metropolis.

The radical nature of the change is briefly expressed in the new slogan, "mission in six continents," which is highly popular today. This slogan may be criticized as blurring outlines and overlooking differences of which account still has to be taken. Mission in the run-down areas of Philadelphia and Chicago may be even more difficult than in Cairo or Bangkok; but the problem of approaching with the Gospel those who have been conditioned all their lives by a non-Christian culture and religion is not the same as that of making the Gospel real to those who live on the margins of a civilization that bears a profound Christian impress. It is misleading when such differences are overlooked. But what the slogan does effectively make clear is that mission is not something that allegedly Christian countries can impose on an unhappy heathen world. Mission is something that all churches are engaged in all the time. Every church, for the sake of its own health, must be both a sending and a receiving church. Wherever a church exists, older or younger, stronger or weaker, richer or poorer, there is the potential center of mission.

It should occasion no surprise that leaders in some younger churches, flushed with their new sense of spiritual freedom, resentful of the patronizing and domineering attitude of some missionaries in the past, and unwilling to risk any encroachments on their hard-won independence, say frankly that now the current should flow in the other direction. The younger churches, with their greater vigor and the freshness of their faith, are now called to help the older churches to recover the vision that they have so largely lost and to become again living members in the body of Christ. Voices such as those of Toyohiko Kagawa, D. T. Niles, and a host of others have aroused the West by their prophetic quality. It is possible gratefully to recognize this new store of spiritual riches which God has given to the churches in our time, and yet to think that the current should still flow in both directions, that the older churches in the West still have a responsibility in relation both to the younger churches and to the non-Christian world which still stands outside the sphere of Christian influence.

We have been accustomed to think of mission as something that happens very far away. The missionary has been romanticized by distance; when he revisits his homeland, he brings with him a certain aura of adventure and heroism. It is not always easy to realize that now the waves of mission wash upon our own front doorstep, or in certain cases, that we have moved our doorstep to the edge of the pool of mission.

A century ago the non-Caucasian student in a Western university was a rarity. When the first Indian student arrived in Cambridge (England) in the 1870's, he was immensely popular and was regarded by his fellow-students as a kind of mascot.[2] Joseph Hardy Neesima, who managed to escape illegally from Japan in 1864 and to study at Amherst College, was in his day a notable phenomenon. Now there are many thousands of students from the mainly non-Christian countries of the world in the universities of the West, as well as a few Western students in the universities of the East. Some are Christians; the majority are non-Christians. Do they get converted? It should be ten times easier to convert a Muslim in America, where he is surrounded by every kind of Christian influence, than to convert the same Muslim in Iran, in the midst of his own family and under the weight of the age-long traditions of a non-Christian faith. This is an area of mission in which the Western churches do not seem to have been conspicuously successful.

Exchange of populations works in the other direction also. More Westerners are living outside their own countries than ever before in the history of the world. When the British authorities withdrew from India in 1947, it was assumed that the number of British people in India would rapidly decrease. To everyone's astonishment this diminution did not take place. Apart from the army, which naturally disappeared, the British population began to increase. Wherever some great project is in hand—the building of a vast bridge or dam, the creation of a new aircraft industry, the con-

2. I was told this by Sir J. J. Thomson, Master of Trinity College, who was born in 1856.

struction of a steel factory—the foreigner is certain to be present. Since Israel has no colonial past, Israeli technicians are particularly welcome in the African countries. The Chinese Communists have undertaken to build the thousand miles of railway which will provide landlocked Zambia with a new outlet to the sea for its almost unlimited store of copper.

Some students of missions, a little dazzled by this multiplication of foreigners abroad, have placed great hopes in the witness abroad of the Christian who is not a professional missionary. The full-time missionary is always somewhat under suspicion as a propagandist whose aim is the substitution of an alien culture and religion for that which previously obtained. The Christian technician, who understands his work in the harnessing of a great river to fertilize the desert and to enrich the life of men as cooperation with the purpose of God and who carries out his duties in the spirit of integrity and humility which are required of the Christian, is in a far stronger position than the professional to bear an uninhibited Christian witness. On such men must rest our hopes for the missionary work of the future.

Certainly this new arm of the Christian endeavor should be taken very seriously. Foreigners with technical competence can live and work in areas such as Afghanistan where no Christian worker as such is admitted. At the same time it is well to notice the limitations under which such men and women are likely to have to work.

Most of those engaged in special projects find themselves living in a village or township constructed by their company or by the local government for the benefit of foreign employees. Everything is planned to be as much like "home" as possible. An enclosed community is built up, and there is only a minimum of contact with the people of the land. The Russians are the worst. For obvious reasons they are under strict control and are not encouraged to make any contacts at all outside their own limited circle, except for purely business reasons. Next come the Germans, who are particularly good at making a little Germany away from home, with a German school, a German church, and of course a German beer garden. But neither the British nor the Americans have much claim in this regard to throw stones at their continental neighbors. The result of this isolation is that the technical expert overseas has few opportunities of friendly contact with colleagues among the local people. Especially in countries where women play little part in social life and public affairs, the difficulty experienced in getting beyond formal and official relationships may prove to be formidable. Added to this is the problem that few among such experts remain more than three years in any one country; few are likely to be successful in mastering more than the rudiments of the language, and contacts are therefore limited to the already Westernized members of the local staff. The value of Christian character shown in integrity and humanity cannot be overestimated; only in exceptional circumstances can Christian witness be expanded beyond this silent form.

In one field, however, the possibilities of the twentieth century far exceed those of the nineteenth. In all the newly independent countries there is a passion for education; but in Africa it is at present difficult to persuade African graduates of the local or Western universities to engage in teaching. The salaries they can command in government service or in commerce are so far beyond the highest that they can hope for in education, and the pressure of the family to secure the highest salary possible is so strong, that the majority, even of those who have been trained as teachers by the government, the moment they have completed their five-year contract disappear from the schools into some more lucrative form of employment. In consequence there is an immense demand for the foreigner who is willing to spend some years in developing secondary education in these countries. In one prosperous secondary school in western Uganda there is not a single African teacher. This is bad, in that there are no wise Africans on the staff to guide the pupils in their difficult transition from the still simple life of an African village to all the complexities of the modern world. It does, however, provide the young Christian from the West who is not a missionary with an opportunity for service at a crucial point in the development of the younger nations.

Naturally not all these schools are of a single type, and consequently the possibilities for direct Christian witness vary from nothing through qualified approval to almost unrestricted freedom. Some schools have grown out of missionary initiative, and the distinctively Christian tradition is maintained. Kenya seems inclined to hold fast to the tradition of religious instruction in the schools. In other areas Christian activities may be limited to the periods out of school. In yet others close relations of friendship between teachers and taught may be discouraged. In time these possibilities will wither away. As the new universities produce an increasing number of graduates, employment in the well-rewarded fields will become less of a certainty, and more graduates will be driven into the field of teaching. It is to be hoped that many among these will be convinced Christians. But for at least a generation we may expect to find here an almost unrestricted sphere in which service can be rendered by the older to the younger churches.

Our attention has so far been directed to what may be called supplementary fields and service at a greater or less distance from the central work of the church in worship, preaching, and witness. Can we still expect that there will be a place for the foreigner in this central work in any part of the world?

The answer is given by the plain fact that one-third of the population of the world has not yet heard the name of Jesus Christ. The greater part of the missionary work that ought to be carried on is still pioneer work. Half of these untouched peoples live in countries, such as China, which are no longer accessible to the missionary from the West. Increasingly the burden must be taken up by the younger churches themselves. But the day of the Western missionary is not yet done.

Nepal was opened to Christian penetration as recently as 1952. This fascinating country, with a population of ten million, wedged between India and China and containing many of the highest mountains in the world, had for centuries tried to keep itself isolated from the rest of the world. Then in 1952 an almost peaceful revolution took place. The king decided to get rid of the prime minister, whose family had for a long time reduced the kings to the role of merely formal ruling, and at the same time set in motion the process of modernizing his country. Part of this liberalizing policy was the permission accorded to Christian missions to develop professional and technical services.

It might be thought that this challenge should have been taken up in the first place by the Indian churches. But this simple suggestion overlooks a difficulty. In Nepal the Indian is as much a foreigner as the American and is likely to be under even deeper suspicion of imperialistic aims. Nepal is fanatically determined to guard its independence; but a country with ten million people is not unnaturally anxious when it finds itself sandwiched between a neighbor on the south with a population of five hundred million, and a neighbor on the north with seven hundred million people.

Indians have not always been sufficiently circumspect in their relationships with this proud and slightly suspicious neighbor.

So for the moment Western missions have considerable liberty. They are not allowed to open stations in the highlands, for instance, among the interesting Sherpa people, well-known to the world for the help they have rendered to generations of Everest climbers, since these are thought to be dangerously near the Chinese frontier. But American Jesuits maintain in Khatmandu, the capital, what is undoubtedly the best school in the country. The Nepal United Mission and the Nepal Evangelistic Band have set up between them a first-rate technical institution, two agricultural projects, five hospitals and a leprosarium. The limitation on their work is that it is still forbidden for a Nepali to change his religion, and any Nepali who is baptized knows well that by taking this step he is running the risk of imprisonment. Yet, in spite of all hindrances, a tiny Nepali church is coming into existence and growing inconspicuously from day to day. One of the last geographical frontiers of the Christian Church has been crossed.

This is perhaps the most sensational new adventure of the Christian forces. But Nepal is by no means the only part of the world in which pioneer missionary work is to be done. The first scientific survey of the Christian situation in Africa showed that, as a result of a century of Christian penetration there was hardly one of the 742 [3] tribes south of the Sahara which had not been in some measure touched by Christianity. But in the case of many of these tribes the Christian influence is thin and superficial. For instance, among the Fon, a tribe in the former French colony of Dahomey numbering a million, there are only a handful

3. These are the tribes recognized as such by ethnologists; if subtribes, some of which have mutually unintelligible forms of speech, are included, the number is upward of three thousand.

of Protestants and a rather larger number of Roman Catholics; it was reckoned that 600,000 people, equal in number to the population of Nevada and Wyoming together, not merely had never heard the Gospel but were not in a position to hear it if they wished.

At a meeting of the All-Africa Church Conference held in Yaoundé in the Cameroons the suggestion was made that the French-speaking Protestant churches of the world should be invited to join in sending an ecumenical team to attempt to Christianize the life of this tribe on every level. The leadership should be African, but appeals for help were sent to countries as far apart as Madagascar and Tahiti, and no embargo was placed on the participation of members of the white races. After one year's training the members of the team have begun work in their allotted area; it is as yet too early to report on the success of their efforts.

Clearly those who promoted this effort were thinking in terms of the comprehensive mission, which believes in the presentation of the Gospel on all levels of human life and in act no less than in word. They could have made their own the words written a generation ago by an ardent supporter of this view:

> Under this approach, evangelization is cure of sick bodies, of broken-down, inefficient and eroded farms, of illiteracy, of insufficient and unbalanced diet, insanitary homes, impure drinking water, of a subsistence level of existence, of filthy villages, of the moral, mental and spiritual stagnation of corrupt practices and conditions. Every effort upon this wide and comprehensive front of Christian service is a part of the Evangel and is required to enable the individual to reach the fulness of stature which is in Christ.[4]

But Merle Davis, who wrote these words, would not for a

4. J. Merle Davis, *New Buildings on Old Foundations* (New York, London, 1947), p. 233.

moment have denied that the central aim of missionary work is direct confrontation with Jesus Christ, such as will lead to living faith in him, and that this faith more than any other thing is the power which makes possible the fullness of human existence.

Only the completion of a careful survey will reveal how many areas there are in Africa where the very foundations of Christian witness still have to be laid. The answer is likely to be more than a hundred. This might well demand of the churches of the world the addition of two thousand new skilled missionaries and at least an equal number of trained African colleagues to the existing force before the end of the century. Of course, in every case the leadership should be African. The basis of the mission should be ecumenical in the sense that its aim is not to reproduce in Africa the minutiae of Western church organization but to bring into being what from the start will be genuinely an African church. Plans must be made to hand over to the local Christians at the earliest possible date full responsibility for the maintenance and the propagation of the faith. The foreigner must go to the work consciously as the servant and helper of the African church.

The progress made by the younger churches is such that if, as in China, all help from outside was cut off, they would for the most part be able to maintain themselves in being and to progress. But many of them will admit that there are certain things that they cannot yet do as well as they should and for which the help of friends from the older churches is still needed.

The area in which this help is still most evidently needed is that of administration. In many areas competent secretaries, treasurers, and accountants are worth their weight in gold. It is not so much that such people do not exist among the members of the churches as that the churches simply cannot afford to employ them. As with teachers, the salaries they can command elsewhere are so high that great personal sacrifice would be involved if they were to accept service with the church. It used to be thought that the worker from overseas was an expensive luxury; now it seems that he is becoming an economy! Not long ago, when a new editor was required for a Christian journal in an African country, it was found that an African editor would expect twice the salary for which a British missionary would be ready to serve.

Another area in which the West will have to stand by for a considerable period is theological education. Few among the younger churches are as yet able to meet from their own resources the demand for competent theological teachers. This is in part our fault. We have allowed theological training to fall behind in the rapid development of education in other fields, with the result that in many areas we have produced the dangerous situation in which the laity are better educated than the ministers. In part, however, the fault is that of the younger churches themselves; economic and family pressure on the educated young man is intense, and in many cases the church, so far from encouraging a promising young man to study theology and to enter the ministry, has directed his hopes towards another and financially more rewarding career. The result is that the ranks of those from whom theological teachers could be drawn are far too thin.

It would be possible to list other fields in which Western help is still needed. But a prior question may already arise in the mind of the reader: Do they want us, or are we still as in the past imposing unwanted guests on unwilling hosts?

That is one of the questions to which it is impossible to give an answer in a single sentence. It is likely that any answer given will be in part conditioned by the generation to which our informant belongs.

In the early days of the missions, tension rarely arose between missionaries and converts. The convert had little desire to concern himself with questions of administration and finance and was quite happy to leave these to his missionary friends. As soon, however, as an organized church began to come into existence, the better-educated Christians started to raise the question, "To whom does the church belong?" Questions of this kind were being asked in Christian conferences in India as early as 1862. Unfortunately there is always a tendency as a church grows for the missionary who starts as the preacher of the Gospel to be transformed into the man who sits in an office and sees to it that other people work. The missionary society appears at a distance not as a body of earnest men concerned about the spread of the Gospel but as an alien corporation the main purpose of which is to keep control of the purse-strings and of the directive power. The missionary is often afraid to lose control and to hand over to untried leaders in the church an authority which it is not certain they will be able to exercise wisely. Those leaders are convinced of their capacity to run everything successfully and regard the missionary as an uncomfortable and unnecessary obstacle in the way of their complete independence.

Clearly, in this situation painful and unpleasant rivalries can arise. But the current of missionary history has already become plain—sooner or later the younger churches must become completely independent and free to exercise their liberty under what they believe to be the guidance of the Holy Spirit. Sometimes liberty is violently thrust upon the churches by political circumstances, as on the churches in Indonesia when the Japanese flood swept away all the western landmarks. More often the revolution has come about quietly and gradually by a process of continuous change. However, this does not alter the fact that it is a revolution. But having attained independence, do they still want missionaries?

We can understand why some who have lived through the period of rivalry will answer with a resounding No! "No more missionaries! This is our church, and we will run it. Western man is incurably obsessed by the desire to dominate; if we let him in, it will not be long before he wants to turn the clock back and run the whole show just as he did before liberation took place." This is the extreme position. We can understand the psychological as well as the historical grounds on which such a decision rests.

But running a large church is not quite as easy as might at first appear, especially when the missionaries have been slow to train younger church leaders in the responsible exercise of authority. This was the state of the great Batak Church in Sumatra some years after the Republic of Indonesia had come into existence. Gradually and hesitantly that church began to consider the admission of a small number of missionaries to work in particular fields, such as theological training, in which the church felt itself to be still weak. But it was made clear that the foreigner must keep strictly to his appointed job; in no circumstances should he be allowed to acquire any influence in the affairs of the church as such.

Now, however, a new generation is growing up which has never known anything but freedom and to which the tensions and resentments of the past mean little. India has been politically independent for twenty-three years; in many areas the church was ahead of the state in committing itself to the policy of independence. A man who today is thirty years old has few, if any memories, of the period before freedom came. Independence is something that he takes for granted; he does not live in a perpetual state of anxiety as to whether it is being threatened.

At the same time a change seems to be taking place in the understanding of the term "church." The older generation was inclined to think of the church as that already existing entity, with church buildings and schools and hospitals, over which it was essential that they themselves should win control. Their children see the church as an expanding body, responsible on every level for the well-being of the society by which it is surrounded. This younger group is able to take seriously the challenge presented by the Whitby Missionary Conference of 1947, the first at which representatives of older and younger churches met on a level of full and unquestioned equality. The question put to the leaders of the younger churches was this—"Tell us what plans you have for the total evangelization of your countries, and let us know at what points we can still help?" It can be taken for granted that the 3 percent of Indians who are Christians will be able to maintain themselves under all imaginable conditions. The question is how they propose to bring the Gospel home to the 97 percent who are not yet Christian. It was clear that in 1947 only the Koreans were thinking in terms of total evangelization.

Nationalism has its drawbacks; it has also certain advantages. A younger generation has been trained to look at the problems of each country as a whole. Such training makes it easy for young Christians to think not in terms of the sectional interests of the Christian Church as it now exists, but of the whole nation as the field which is to be penetrated on every level by the Gospel. Some, indeed, are looking beyond the limits of their own nation and thinking in terms of an even wider area. In Southeast Asia there is an active process of exchange under which Asian Christians go to work in countries other than their own. It is clear that, if the work of total evangelization is to be carried out by the existing churches unaided, it will take a very long time. If it can be speeded up by judicious help from the West, what have the younger churches to be afraid of? Their governments are eager to welcome the help of international teams of experts, for instance, to help in stamping out malaria; why should the churches be afraid of international help in carrying out their far greater campaigns?

Such utterances are to be heard mainly on the lips of the under-thirties in the churches. But there are signs that this is the generation to which we in the West should be increasingly prepared to listen. If we inquire of them, as I have, rather than of published material or official declarations of the churches, we receive some unexpected replies.

Our first question, then, is, "If you want missionaries from abroad, what do you want them for?" The surprising answer is, "For everything! Of course a missionary must be able to do something exceptionally well. In certain pioneer areas of the world nothing more is needed even today than deep piety and the willingness to endure hardship. But in most churches the missionary will have to hold his own with highly qualified Christians and non-Christians of our race; if he is not really up to the job, he will always feel painfully embarrassed and inferior."

Nor need it be supposed that the missionary will always be the underdog. Equality in service means also equality in opportunity and privilege. The foreigner may well find himself elected by the younger church to the top job in its service. Interesting examples of this can be cited from among the most advanced of the younger churches. The Tamil Evangelical Lutheran Church, having had its first distinguished Indian bishop Dr. Rajah B. Manikam, decided that it would be for the good of the church that the next bishop should be a Swede. As the rule of the church required, the names of three candidates—all Swedes—were sent into Sweden, and one of them, a highly experienced missionary, Dr. C. G. Diehl, was chosen to be bishop. In a diocese of the Church of South India the electoral body voted three times and came out with a solid majority in favor of a missionary of the London Missionary Society; it could not agree on an Indian name to stand with his. As the rule requires, however, that two names must be submitted to the synod committee which makes the final choice, that committee was able to quash the election and to appoint an Indian who was entirely unknown to the diocese which he was to serve. If such an electoral body is criticized for retrograde action in choosing a foreigner rather than a national, it is likely to reply with some disgust: "You gave us our spiritual freedom, didn't you? Who are you to object if we use our liberty to follow the guidance of the Holy Spirit, and to choose the man whom we have been led to regard as best qualified to do the job?"

Our next question will be, "We have been told that you want only experts, who will stay for a short time and then move on. Is this your view?" It is at this point that the answer which is now beginning to be heard is the most surprising of all: "We want missionaries who will lay their bones here." The expert who comes for two or three years to do a particular job is invaluable. But it takes a long time for a foreigner really to become accustomed to the ways of a people and of a church to which he does not belong by birth. Most of those who have done outstanding work have been those who have gradually learned to accept the land of their exile as their home.

"Can you then," we may go on to ask, "give us some picture of the kind of missionaries that you would like us to send you?" Here the answers will vary according to area and to the age of the church from which our interlocutor comes. But four points are likely to recur in almost every answer.

The foreigner must come as the servant of the church and not as its boss. He must not be afraid to exercise leadership, if he is called to it by the church which he serves. But he must never forget that he is a guest, and that the initiative must always lie on the side of the church. This is harder than it sounds. The white man tends to be rapid in decision and prompt in action. Unless he is watchful, others out of politeness or indifference will allow him to have his way, when the interests of the church would have been better served if he had learned to exercise patience and to wait.

He must of course identify himself with the church and the people whom he serves. This is far more a matter of attitude and of psychological approach than of external details of dress and personal habits. It is important that the missionary should be able gracefully to accept the hospitality of friends whose tradition differs from his own; but it is far better that he should not pretend that he is not what he is—a foreigner. Nor should he be afraid of saying straight out, but courteously, what is in his mind. "Our fathers were inclined to regard criticism as a sign of hostility or racial superiority; we recognize it as something from which we can learn. To us the white man who thinks that the black man is always right is as much a nuisance as the old type which assumed that the black man was always wrong."

The missionary must have no doubt as to the purpose for which he has come overseas. He must be a missionary. That means that, waking or sleeping, he must be dominated by one central concern—that men and women should be brought to know Jesus Christ and to find life in him. This does not mean that he is to be an unscrupulous propagandist. If his job is to teach history in a college, then he must teach history up to the highest possible level of academic excellence and impartiality. But all the time he will be conscious of his students as human beings for whom Christ died. If he does not measure up to this demand, he had better stay at home.

"The missionary must be the kind of man or woman in whom we can see Jesus Christ." The young leader in the church knows well that it cannot bear effective witness unless it manifests the lineaments of Jesus of Nazareth who made himself the Servant of us all. He is horrified at the "image" which the church has all too often presented in the past—as the doorway to foreign infiltration, as the destroyer of inherited values, as a mutual insurance society, the major concern of which appears to be jobs for the boys, as a body the professions of which bear little relation to its practice. He is distressed by the low level of spiritual life with which all too many in the church are content. Many of the older leaders seem to have become so involved in ancient rivalries or in the daily tasks of administration as to have lost the power to inspire. The foreigner stands outside all this; just because he is a foreigner, he is no partisan, unless he foolishly makes himself one, in the local intrigues and strivings for power. He comes from a church with a far longer tradition of Christian life and spirituality. Can he manifest the likeness of Christ, perhaps without words spoken, in such a way that those who meet him will know that he dwells deep and will be led to say with the Shunammite woman of old, "Behold now, I perceive that this is a holy man of God, who is continually passing our way" (2 Kings 4:9)?

This is an alarming, indeed a terrifying, ideal with which to be confronted. Yet it is in essence simply the challenge by which every Christian is confronted everywhere, in all circumstances and all the time. In a still largely non-Christian country the challenge presses with special intensity only because the supporting forces are so weak, and the opposing forces are felt to be stronger than anywhere in the nominally Christian world. The question is simply one of obedience. There are jobs waiting to be done. No one Christian has a right to say to any other, "This and no other is the job that you ought to be doing." But equally no Christian has a right to say, "This is a job which I will not in any circumstances consider." It might, after all, be precisely the job for which the Lord of all life had been preparing him from the day of his birth. The old word of Scripture still stands "His mother said to the servants, 'Do whatever he tells you'" (John 2:5). When the servants obey the word spoken, the Lord himself is present to confirm the word with signs following.